LORRIES OF ARABIA 3

ERF NGC

Robert Hackford

LORRIES OF ARABIA 3

ERF NGC

Robert Hackford

Lorries of Arabia 3

Old Pond Publishing is an imprint of Fox Chapel Publishers International Ltd.

Project Team
Vice President–Content: Christopher Reggio
Associate Publisher: Sarah Bloxham
Layout: David Exley, www.beamreachuk.co.uk
Photos as credited in the text

ISBN 978-1-912158-36-2

A catalogue record for this book is available from the British Library.

Fox Chapel Publishing
903 Square Street
Mount Joy, PA 17552, USA

Fox Chapel Publishers International Ltd.
7 Danefield Road, Selsey (Chichester)
West Sussex PO20 9DA, U.K.

www.oldpond.com

We are always looking for talented authors. To submit an idea, please send a brief inquiry to acquisitions@foxchapelpublishing.com.

Printed and bound in China
22 21 20 19 2 4 6 8 10 9 7 5 3 1

CONTENTS

ABOUT THE AUTHOR

(Photo: Gary Corbishley)

Robert Hackford (born 1952) started out as a school teacher, progressing to a headship quite early on. However, mid-career he opted for a change and became a TIR driver instead. After doing Europe for a while, a trip to Turkey whetted his appetite for long-haul work and he subsequently spent a number of years driving to North Africa. He made a handful of Astran trips to the Arabian Gulf driving an Iveco Eurostar with a manual constant-mesh gearbox, as far afield as Doha in Qatar. For Robert, each new trip was an adventure with a sense of achievement at the end of it. He even ran his own unit and trailer for a while. During the '90s he often wrote articles for the various truck magazines. Robert returned to teaching, first in Istanbul then Rome and eventually in Cairo where he served as the head of a British International School before retiring in 2014. He is the author of *Lorries of Arabia: ERF NGC*, published by Old Pond in 2015; and *Lorries of Arabia 2: ERF NGC*, published in 2016.

ACKNOWLEDGEMENTS

Marc Van Steenbergen: Belgian haulier. Wobbe Reitsma, Hans Witte: Dutch transport historians. Rene Tanner: Swiss transport historian. Ken Broster: former general manager for Trans Arabia in Jeddah. Gary Corbishley: restorer and owner of KCH 95N. Rene Postma: erstwhile owner of the same unit. Jerry Cooke: former NGC driver and mechanic for Trans Arabia. Vince Cooke: former S Jones driver. Bill Fitzsimons: former ERF field engineer. Dave Wallace: former NGC driver for John Simmons. John Davies: mechanic for Trans Arabia. Mick Jones: Trans Arabia. Alan Rickett: ERF publicity officer. Chris Jeffries: operations manager and ex-driver at Eric Vick. Manal Maseras: transport artist. Graham Beech, Roy Mead, Pod Robinson, Adrian Cyper, 'Chepstowechap', Ady Goodman, Paul Gee, Gerdi Kimpe, David Pilcher, Mark Bailey, Bjorn Kjer, Ted Croswell, Stephen John Heward, Alan Ball: transport photographers.

In particular, I wish to acknowledge Dean Bartlett, an international driver and blogging transport historian, for his tireless research efforts in support of this volume.

(Photo: Dave Wallace)

(Photo: Alan Rickett)

INTRODUCTION: ERF'S LONG-HAUL PIONEER

(Photo: ERF promo)

The gentleman standing next to the NGC in the picture above is Peter Foden, who was the man in charge when the model was conceived.

The rugged NGC 'European' 42-tonner with its Cummins 335, 9-speed Fuller 'box, left-hand drive and legendary reliability was ERF's flash of brilliance. Herewith, my third book on this subject, in which I continue to narrate an unfolding history of a premium tractive unit model that for some years lay forgotten in time. As with the second book in this series, I have carefully avoided repetition. Where I have broached previously mentioned subjects, I have done so only to provide context for newly discovered material. This volume provides new details, new findings, new insights and new pictures relating to the ERF NGC. Since the previous books, evidence of most, if not all, of the 91 NGCs known to have been built have come to light. These can be found in the revised NGC register at the back of this volume.

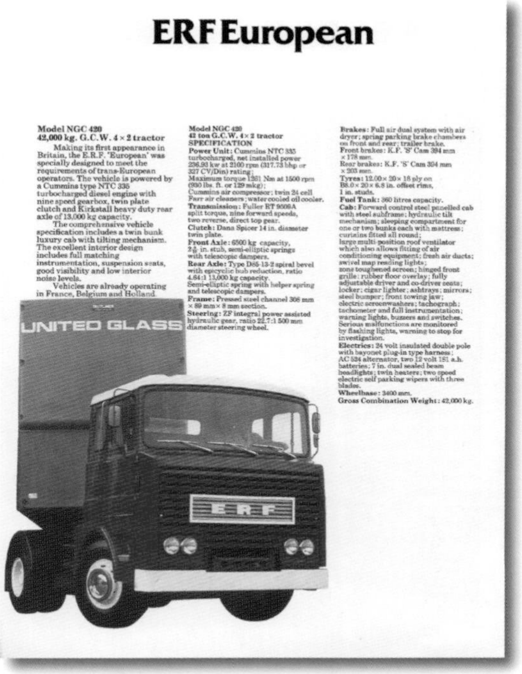

Usually, when writing a monograph about a vintage lorry, history throws up more and more variants of that model, the deeper one delves. Remarkably, the more I researched the NGC model for this *Lorries of Arabia: ERF NGC* series, the simpler and cleaner its specification became, thus resulting in fewer variants. Indeed, the NGCs that left ERF's factory in Sandbach have proved to be far more uniform than I was originally led to believe when I was researching Book 1. Of course, the working histories of each individual unit appeared progressively more complicated the more I probed, but that is a separate issue.

(From ERF Earls Court 1974 brochure)

For a start, many of the variants and options suggested in ERF's brochures never reached fruition – there were in practice no NGCs with straight-framed chassis or Gardner engines, for example. Furthermore, all the 6x4 examples have been shown to be retrospective; none having left the factory with double-drive. Indeed, only three of the NGCs known at the time of writing were converted from standard 4x2 NGCs. One of these was the vehicle supplied to Cauvas in France (pictured in Book 1), which we now know was supplied in 4x2 form and converted to 6x4 later (more details of this in the European section).

This makes the standard ERF NGC a very pure breed indeed: LHD, tilting 7MW sleeper cab, 14-litre Cummins NTC 335 engine, 9-speed Fuller 'box and D85 hub-reduction rear axle. All were Euro-spec (and were therefore all 'Europeans'); and all were 4x2 (6x4s were later conversions). Basically, there was just a standard NGC unit.

The only factory variant was the relatively rare NGC with a Cummins 290 lump with a 13-speed Fuller, and reports of two having been fitted with naturally aspirated NHC 250s. I find this degree of uniformity in an ERF model of the period quite remarkable, especially as all of its many '70s stablemates had a wide range of significant variations regarding chassis options, cabs, engines, gearboxes, LHD/RHD, UK-spec/Euro-spec, etc.

(Photo: ERF promo)

The ERF NGC with its taller, roomier, better appointed tilting 7MW cab simply overtook 5MW versions from 1973 onwards, though the cheaper 5MW options remained available alongside both the NGC 'European' and the B-series.

When it came to competing with the opposition for a long-haul 1970s tractive unit, ERF definitely got it right the first time round with this great British-built/assembled icon of early trans-European trucking.

I am sometimes asked why I chose to write books only about the ERF NGC – the one with the boxy 7MW cab – and not about all the other Motor Panels MW-cabbed ERF models with the squatter, more rounded fixed (non-tilting) cab with the split windscreen. Good question. The fact is, as previously stated, the NGC model had almost no variants. The smaller, rounded cab models with the split windscreen, however, are a proper minefield but deserve one day to be written about. There were several variants of that short Motor Panels Mk 4 cab (3MW/5MW, 4MW/6MW, etc.); there were two different front axle positions; there were several variants of chassis (including the RHD 5MW-cabbed

(Photo: Advert from **TRUCK** *magazine)*

A-series); there were 4x2 or 6x4 options; there were RHD or LHD options; there were at least seven different engine options in various capacities from Cummins, Rolls Royce and Gardner; there were at least four different gearbox options in various configurations from David Brown and Fuller; there were light or heavy options; and models could be spec'd differently for European export, Middle East export, New Zealand export or domestic UK use.

(Photo: Martin Phippard/Richard Stanier collection)

In the end I firmly decided to stick only with the NGC for my books as it was certainly the tidier project and in any case it fulfilled my original mission to demonstrate that it was a premium long-hauler. It was, too, a significantly different model from the earlier models, having been designed by ERF's then recently appointed chief engineer, Jack Cooke. Indeed, one of the comments Pat Kennett made in his 1975 Euro-Test, which included an ERF NGC, for *TRUCK* magazine was, 'It's hard to recognise the ERF European as being based on the old familiar Motor Panels steel cab structure. If the Sandbach engineers can make such a good job of this cab, imagine what they'll do with the B-series when the European version appears.'

(Cover of **TRUCK** *magazine)*

The NGC definitely hit the big time when it was featured with a glamour girl on the front page of *TRUCK* magazine! That NGC was shown on stand 87 of the Earls Court show in 1974, about which *Commercial Motor* magazine gave a very useful description in its 20 September issue, as follows:

> The 42-ton-gtw tractive unit, the ERF European, is also new to Earls Court although it made its public debut at the 1973 Brussels Show. The sleeper-type cab is totally different from the B-series, being panelled in steel on a steel sub-frame, and many of these vehicles are already operating in France, Belgium and Holland. The engine is one of the larger Cummins units, the turbocharged NTC 335, which develops 237kW (317 bhp) at 2,100rpm and a maximum torque of 1,261Nm (930 lb ft) at 1,500rpm. The rear axle is of 13-tonne (12.8-ton) capacity while the front is plated at 6.5 tonnes (6.4 tons). Telescopic dampers are specified front and rear. Compared to the normal 270-litre fuel tank on the UK B-series, the European tractor has a capacity of 360 litres (80 gal). The wheelbase is slightly longer at 3.8 m (11 ft 2 in) compared with 3.0 m (9 ft 10 in).

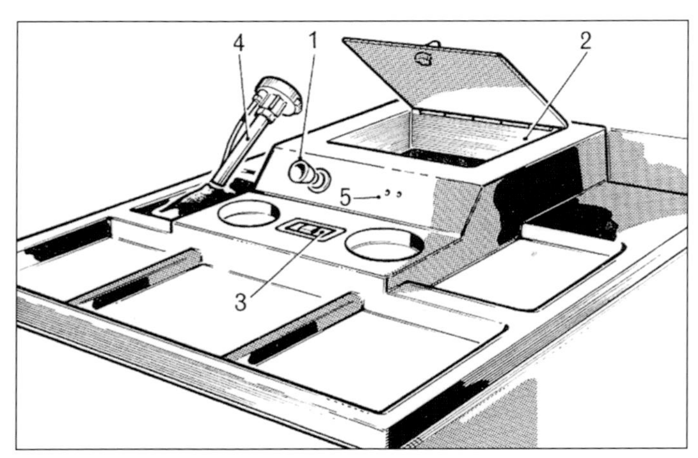

(From ERF handbook)

The drawing above is from the driver's handbook and shows the pre-formed centre console with provision for the reachable storage of a driver's belongings. It incorporated a cigar lighter, lockable glove compartment, map stowage and ash tray. Space was available for the fitting of a shaver power point and hand lamp.

(Photo: ERF promo)

There is a fascinating twenty-minute documentary made by Freelance Directors Productions, called *ERF 1974*, in which the television presenter John Burke interviews Peter Foden about the company. The film also features footage of ERF trucks out on the road – including various LV-cabbed models, fire engines and even a 4MW. Peter Foden mentions that they were struggling to meet demand. The film shows various stages of the production line at Sandbach, including cab and engine installation. There is some marvellous footage of A-series and very early B-series artics undergoing punishing high-speed trials on the MIRA test track and the road haulage proving grounds. Further footage shows the ERF parts workshops at Middlewich. Various still shots of 4/5MW-cabbed units are slipped in.

The most exciting aspect though, for me, was the presence of NGC 'Europeans' throughout the film. A 4x2 tractive unit in primer hovers in the background in some shots and John Burke demonstrates the interior before climbing down. Another NGC in factory 'rocket red' and white is seen in the wind tunnel undergoing fluttering tag and smoke tests. It appears to be a prototype without a roof vent or grille water cap. A third NGC appears, with its grille up, in ERF's service and parts workshop at Middlewich. A still picture of one of Van Steenbergen's NGCs is also screened. Finally, a short road run filmed from the interior of an NGC accompanies a brief interview with one of the testers.

(Photo: Robert Hackford)

A small detail: I have always found that short door an endearing feature. Not many Motor Panels cabs used the short door, most preferring ones that followed the contours of the wheel arch. That short door has a truncated A-shape, echoing the side elevation of the complete cab.

The steel 7MW cab, supplied by Motor Panels of Coventry, was very well appointed for its period. ERF did not buy steel cabs to circumvent German legislation against plastic cabs, as is sometimes thought: those were EEC rules that came into force in 1978, the year following the ERF NGC's demise.

Motor Panels of Coventry made the tall version of its Mark 4 cab for only three models: the ERF NGC, the Scammell Crusader and the French Mack. In practice, the 7MW cab supplied to ERF for the NGC was vastly superior to the other two. For a start, it tilted – and to 68 degrees. Secondly, it was very well appointed within, by any standards of the period. Thirdly, it was less angular, the front grille being more subtly shaped. The big visual difference (from the Mack and Scammell versions) was the odd protruding grille assembly stuck on the front of the ERF. The more I look at it, the more I recognise its harmony with the very attractively designed cab. That ERF 7MW grille was almost imperceptibly bowed outwards at the top and sides. This was clearly echoed by the inner uprights of the grille, which followed its curved contours and were parallel. This means that the cross-slats must have been of very slightly different lengths.

Furthermore, the whole of the protruding grille assembly was bevelled inwards top and sides to produce a slight snout. Photos show how the sides of the protruding grille are angled slightly inwards so that even head-on you can see those sides. The front area of the whole grille appears to be narrower than the cab. ERF's diagrammatic plan bears this out.

The Scammell cab, on the other hand, was altogether more 'macho' with its severely angular grille, split windscreen and austere interior. Impressive though it was in appearance, the Scammell version didn't tilt and had instead a swing-out radiator arrangement.

According to the workshop manual and parts catalogue, the 7MW cab shared most features with the 8MW cab, including its ability to tilt and its LHD orientation. In ERF's cab coding system an even number denoted a cab for a chassis with its wheels set forward. It is thought that the 8MW was built as a loose cab to replace worn or damaged 4MW or 6MW cabs. Being identical to the 7MW, its outward appearance resembled a set-back cab. Therefore, it is most likely that the 8MW's mounting brackets were designed to fit, retrospectively, chassis with wheels set forward. This being the case, the cab front would have been cantilevered out over the front end of the chassis rails, to give the wheels clearance to the front step, requiring some sort of extension bracket arrangement.

The diagram right is from a Motor Panels brochure entitled *European Sleeper Cab* and describes various versions of their Mark 4 cab. It can be seen that the ERF NGC's 7MW cab was derived from their Type 3 version depicted in the diagram.

Elsewhere in the brochure, the following description appears: 'Doors are mounted on out-rigger hinges to permit maximum entry and are fitted with both rotary locks and separate anti-burst metal dove-tails. Twin seals, on inner and outer door faces, ensure a snug, weather-proof cab.'

(From ERF handbook)

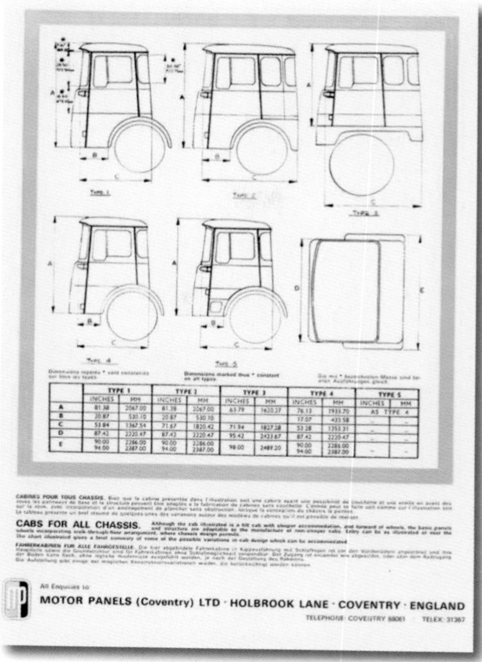

Dimensions marked thus * constant on all types.

	TYPE 1		TYPE 2		TYPE 3		TYPE 4		TYPE 5	
	INCHES	MM	INCHES	MM	INCHES	MM	INCHES	MM	INCHES	MM
A	81.38	2067.00	81.38	2067.00	63.79	1620.27	76.13	1933.70	AS TYPE 4	
B	20.87	530.10	20.87	530.10			17.07	433.58	–	–
C	53.84	1367.54	71.67	1820.42	71.94	1827.28	53.28	1353.31	–	–
D	87.42	2220.47	87.42	2220.47	95.42	2423.67	87.42	2220.47	–	–
E	90.00 94.00	2286.00 2387.00	90.00 94.00	2286.00 2387.00	98.00	2489.20	90.00 94.00	2286.00 2387.00	–	–

CABS FOR ALL CHASSIS. Although the cab illustrated is a tilt cab with sleeper accommodation, and forward of wheels, the basic panels and structure are adaptable to the manufacture of non-sleeper cabs. Entry can be as illustrated or over the wheels incorporating walk-through floor arrangement, where chassis design permits. The chart illustrated gives a brief summary of some of the possible variations in cab design which can be accommodated.

All Enquiries to

MOTOR PANELS (Coventry) LTD · HOLBROOK LANE · COVENTRY · ENGLAND

TELEPHONE COVENTRY 88061 TELEX: 31367

(From Motor Panels brochure)

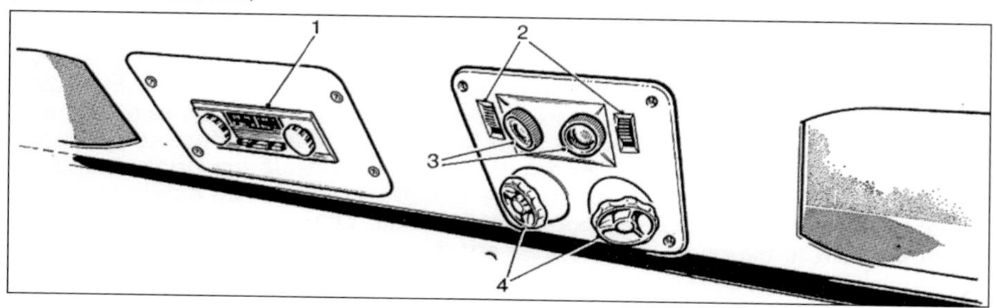

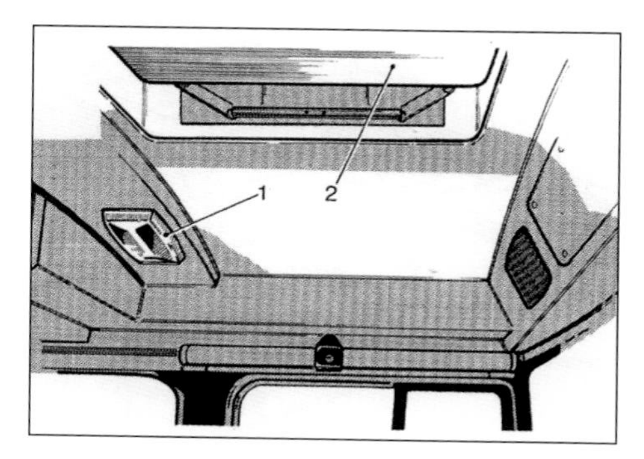

Two details from the driver's handbook showing the airliner-style ventilation nozzles and reading lights above the driver's seat; and the roof hatch that was designed to accommodate an air-conditioning unit such as those manufactured by Kysor. Electrics were by Lucas.

(Photo: Marcus Lester)

It was very significant that Cummins used this NGC as a test bed for the 'big cam' NTE 290 engine. The older 'small cam' NTC 290 and 335 were falling behind the opposition in terms of fuel consumption and the NTE 290 (E for economy) was a huge improvement. 'Big cam' referred to the increase in diameter and profile of the camshaft, which also controls the fuel injection and timing, giving a shorter and sharper injection period.

Predictably, this newer version of the 14-litre straight-six Cummins required a slightly different driving style because there was high torque at even lower revs and it was possible to let the engine lug down to about 1000 rpm before changing down.

HNV 59N was used to haul Cummins's hospitality trailer to events. In *Lorries of Arabia: Part 2,* I argue that it would have been interesting if ERF had continued to market the NGC beyond 1977 using this highly successful engine.

After working for Cummins, HNV 59N spent a brief period in the service of Pountains Heavy Haulage hauling a race-truck trailer all

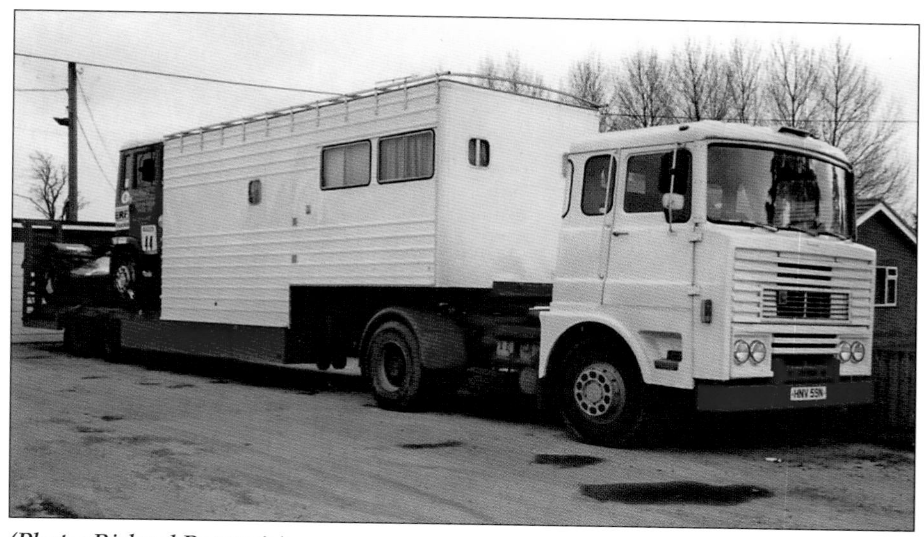

(Photo: Richard Pountain)

over Europe, round the circuits of what was then a popular sport. Richard bought it from Vee & Inline Diesels of Daventry and sold it on to Watts Trucks of Newport, whence it passed on to Redcap Transport (see following photo).

HNV 59N is seen here in the livery of Redcap Transport of Newport. Sometimes nicknamed the 'Sandbach Scania' for its front-end resemblance to that of its contemporary rival, the Scania 140; this example actually carries a cheeky Scania badge! Even as early as the week before the NGC was launched at the Brussels motor show in January 1973, *Commercial Motor* previewed it by mentioning its 'very bold Scania-like grille'! Here, it has been newly painted in the livery of Redcap Transport of Newport. The front towing jaw and heavy steel bumper were standard.

(Photo: 'Chepstowchap')

HNV 59N, having belonged to Cummins engines, Pountains heavy haulage, then Redcap, is seen here in its final scrapped state. My reason for including it is that the picture gives an unusual glimpse of the waisted chassis, which tapered at the end to accommodate the heavy-duty 13-tonne hub-reduction Kirkstall D85 rear axle, which was standard on ERF NGCs. The diagram, from a lubrication chart, shows the chassis shape quite clearly.

ERF's publicity officer appears to have used two or three pictures of this unit taken at Sandbach on much of the early NGC promotional material. It seems likely that this particular unit was a prototype because it lacks the distinctive roof vent and the external water filler cap lid on the grille. ERF's factory colours were 'rocket red' and white and all demo NGCs were presented in that livery; the most spectacular example being JLG 35N, which demonstrated in the Middle East fully kitted out with air-con box, visor and breather-pipes (see later chapter).

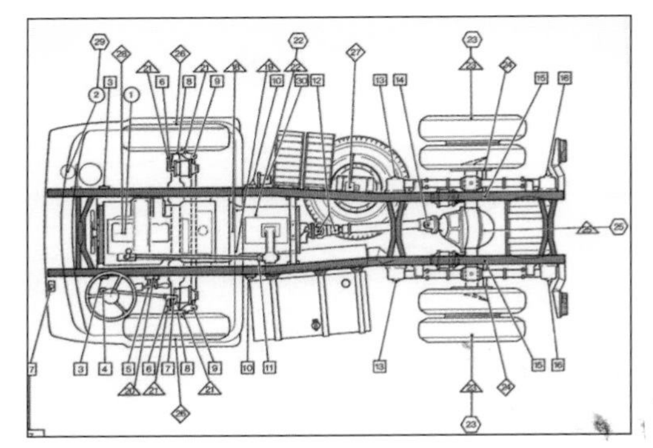

(ERF lubrication chart)

(Photo: Mick Jones)

(Photo: Alan Rickett)

The use of a Boalloy Tautliner trailer with an ERF motor-show demonstrator should surprise no one who remembers the historically close relationship between ERF and Boalloy. However, I cannot think of a less flattering trailer to place behind a new trail-blazing long-hauler than one of United Glass's 4-metre high milk bottle transporters. A TIR tilt would have looked much better in my opinion!

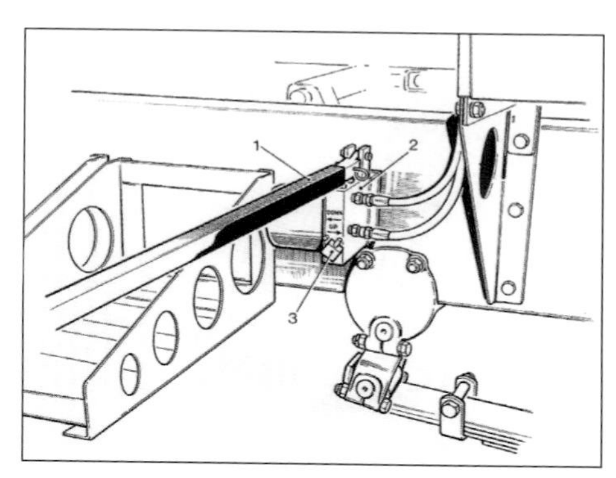

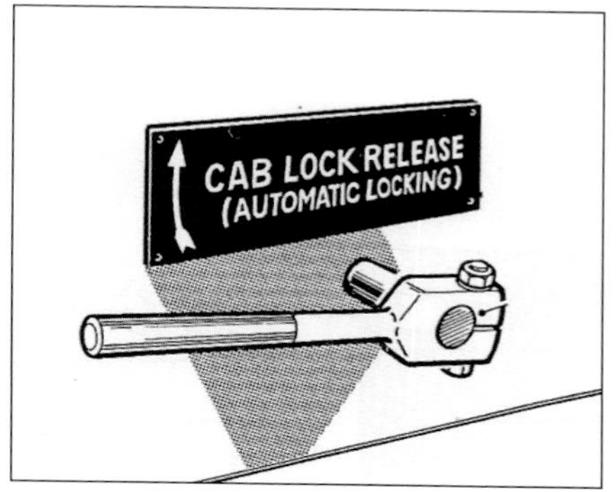

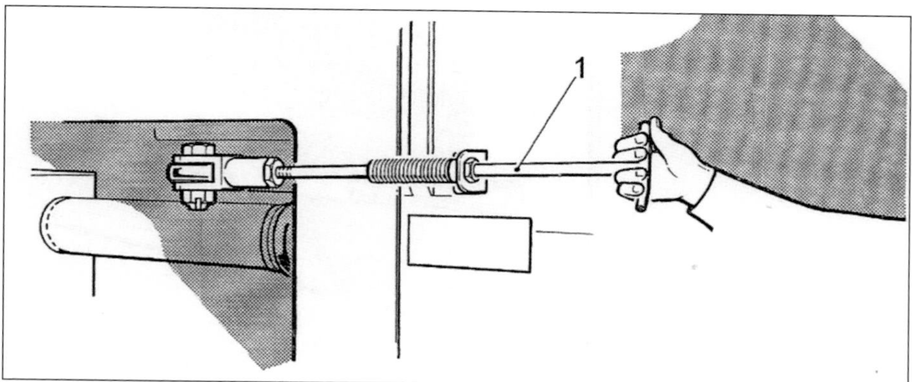

(From ERF handbook)

These three drawings from the driver's handbook show the three-stage locking arrangement for the tilting cab. The first shows the exterior lock behind the cab, the second shows the interior lock; and the third shows the hydraulic hand pump for lifting the cab.

In a sense, ERF simply did what many motor manufacturers do even today: run a limited production line of expensive-to-produce specialist vehicles on the back of high-volume popular models using economy of scale to absorb the cost.

For what it's worth, here's my humble opinion about why the title 'European' wasn't very clear when applied to early 1970s ERFs and why the name was discontinued when the NGC ceased production in 1977.

The NGC was always called the 'European' by ERF and by drivers. However, both the LHD 5MW-cabbed units and early B-series were also occasionally referred to as 'Europeans' in some brochures and articles of the early 1970s. It is my belief that ERF only intended this to apply to those LHD units that were specifically prepared to European specification, meeting EEC requirements. For example, a LHD 5MW supplied to a UK operator for international work would not necessarily be a Euro-spec version or even an export version so it would not, technically, be a 'European'. Besides, ERF was producing LHD versions for countries in the Middle East and Far East that didn't need to meet those European requirements.

The NGC differed from all contemporary ERF models in that it was only ever produced as a fully Europeanised lorry. As Britain entered the EEC in the mid-1970s, the need to distinguish between domestic and Euro-spec lorries became redundant because the UK was by then subject to EEC rules anyway. This would explain why the new full-sized LHD sleeper-cabbed B-series wasn't dubbed a 'European' when it came out in 1976. It would also explain why ERF didn't later use this title for its subsequent LHD E-series and EC-series ranges.

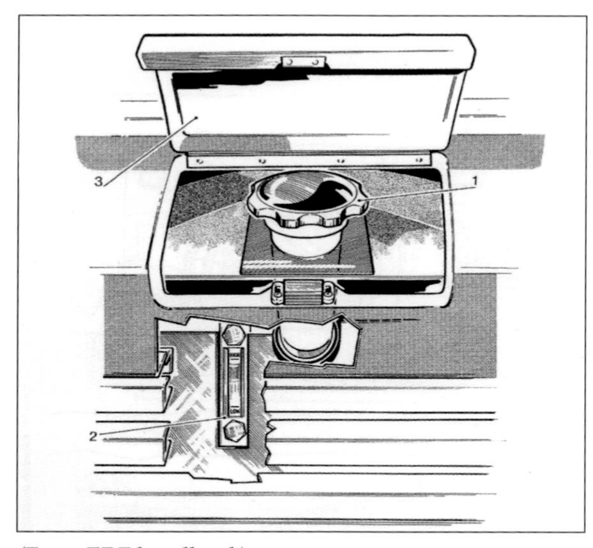

(From ERF handbook)

Nonetheless, for the purposes of this book we can relax in the knowledge that the NGC model absolutely retained its 'European' tag right up to the present time, probably because every single one of them was a Euro-spec LHD vehicle.

The line drawing shows the water filler cap on top of the protruding radiator grille, complete with water gauge. Special consideration was given to all aspects of filtration and cooling, bearing in mind the worldwide application of these vehicles. Twin filters, whilst providing more than adequate air filtration for normal operators, were fully capable of ensuring intake of clean air in dusty conditions. Oil and fuel filtration complied with the exacting requirements of engine manufacturers such as Cummins; and Trans Arabia's mechanics bore testimony to that in Book 2. Pressurised water coolant of ample capacity ensured efficient engine operating temperatures, irrespective of ambient ones.

(Photo: Robert Hackford)

(Photo: Dave Wallace)

The handbrake lever was mounted on the dashboard and the trailer handbrake lever was mounted in the centre console beside the driver. The main unit handbrake on the dashboard appeared in two different forms: a two-stage lift-and-move job, as indicated in the handbook (see diagram on page 26 of *Lorries of Arabia 2*) as seen in this shot; and a chunkier lift-and-turn version. There seems to be no pattern to this, as either appeared on UK and European export models. At the time of writing, it remains a mystery as to why there were two versions.

GEH 513N started out in Beresford livery with a subbie called Albert Dale on Swiss work. It also undertook Middle East work for a short while before it was bought for heavy haulage work by John Simmons, often pulling some considerable weights.

Dave Wallace, who was its regular driver, remembers that the fuel filter used to play up at some awkward moments, including during the ascent of a one-in-seven hill with a crusher. The lorry was grossing 105 tons and the trip was from Enderby to Horton. Having almost reached his destination, a quarry at the summit, in low gear, the fuel filter stopped cooperating just as the road began to level. A six-wheeler

(Photo: Dave Wallace)

tipper got him started again. It's not surprising that drivers always remember that sort of moment!

(Photo: Dave Wallace)

Colin Wallace, who appears in this interior picture of the same unit as pictured above commented, 'Until GEH 513N I'd only ridden in LV and A-series, so the cab seemed huge in comparison. Plus, it had double bunks so my first night out in a cab was in GEH. When you felt the weight it was pulling (some of those draglines and crushers were heavy) you wondered why so many put ERF down.

(Photo: Dave Wallace)

ERF should have released a UK version.' A CB radio with its microphone can be seen above the driver reminding us of this aspect of the era in which NGCs were operated.

The idea of a boy growing up with an ERF NGC is naturally irresistible. Colin was manoeuvring GEH 513N with heavy plant off road at the age of fourteen. His father, Dave, told me that as soon as Colin's feet could reach the pedals there was no holding him back. Brilliant – but how things have changed!

(Photo: 'Chepstowchap')

Dave Wallace reports that the later transplant of a 13-speed Fuller from a Belgian NGC (reported in Book 1) helped considerably because of the high weights they carried.

It is worth noting that only a few NGCs left Sandbach with 13-speed (instead of 9-speed) Fuller gearboxes. Others were retro-fitted, as in this case. NGCs had the type of installation in which the splitter servo was piped directly to the control switch, rather than via the clutch servo. This enabled fast clutch-less split shifts requiring only a brief break in torque load by momentarily lifting the accelerator

(Photo: Dave Wallace)

(as with the later Eaton Twin-splitter), as opposed to requiring use of the clutch for every split shift.

The mastermind behind ERF's '70s flagship was their chief design engineer, Jack Cooke, who joined them in 1971, replacing Alan Turner. He had been engineering director at a rival truck manufacturer, Atkinson, which had recently merged with Seddon to become Seddon-Atkinson. Jack served his apprenticeship at Leyland Motors before joining the RAF as a flight engineer at the start of the Second World War. Later he joined Maudslay Motors as their senior design engineer until 1956, when he went to Atkinson.

In his book *ERF, The Inside Story* Dai Davies describes Jack Cooke as 'an excellent engineer and a fantastic person in every way, easy to get on with and a good listener'. And in an interview with the magazine *Motor Transport* some years later, Jack indicated that he was indeed proud of this trouble-free creation: the NGC.

(Photo: Alan Rickett)

I once read a truck-tester's report on the Volvo FH in which he said 'the cab oozed quality'. Upon reading this I immediately thought, 'Well, that's exactly how I felt about my first experience of an ERF NGC.' It was a superbly crafted machine, 'gaffer's motor' be damned!

In his editorial comments in *TRUCK* magazine in June 1975, Pat Kennett said, 'We do not subscribe to the myth that certain imported trucks are better than the domestic product, a myth that has been fostered by some publications, and apparently swallowed by some operators. That we had the courage to support our convictions is shown by the fact we included a British truck in our selection for the European Super-truck test, reported in this issue. That truck was an ERF. We were not the least bit surprised when it proved more than equal to the challenge. ERF's own engineers were not surprised either.' And as we know that ERF was an NGC.

(Advert from TRUCK *magazine)*

WHY WASN'T A DOMESTIC RIGHT-HAND DRIVE NGC PRODUCED?

(Photo: Richard Pountain)

This picture shows a RHD ERF MDC 852 that was recabbed with a 7MW (or possibly an 8MW) after its 6MW cab was accident damaged and I include it simply to show what a RHD NGC might have looked like. We may never discover the real answer to the question of why a domestic RHD NGC was never produced, as it seems not to have been recorded. The answer may indeed be an entirely political one resulting from decisions made behind closed doors. In this section I examine

(Advert from **TRUCK** *magazine)*

some theories as to why, in practice, such vehicles were not developed.

In Book 2, I explored the idea of a UK version of the NGC but was unable to account for ERF's reluctance to create one. A fascinating letter written by D.A. Oulten, who had worked in the Jennings workshop at ERF, appeared in *Heritage Commercials* magazine (December 2016) recounting an overheard conversation between Peter Foden and a customer who wanted to order a substantial number of UK-spec NGCs but was told that none would be built for UK roads. I will explore possible reasons for this.

But first, by way of background, the following advertisement reminds us that ERF was targeting international operators, not domestic ones.

Traders of the Lost Marque! Other ERF dealerships that we know handled NGCs included Richard Read of Longhope and Beech's Garage in Hanley. This advert is from the June 1975 issue of *TRUCK* magazine. Maybe it's no coincidence that this was the same issue that reported the famous Euro Test in which the ERF NGC 'European' outperformed its Continental rivals! Nonetheless, the advert is another fascinating piece of social history, reflecting the mid-'70s 'Buy British' campaign. This was an attempt to raise the ERF NGC 'European', which had previously been only available as an export lorry, above the parapet to appeal to British operators on international work.

This advert was clearly aimed at patriotic UK hauliers but protectionism was increasingly perceived as being at odds with the spirit of the EEC, which Britain had only just joined, on this side of the Channel, and by June 1975, British hauliers on international work were already shopping elsewhere – it seems that no matter how good the ERF NGC was, it had missed the boat.

However, little interest appears to have been shown by UK operators in this particular model for a number of possible reasons. Firstly, ERF's NGC wasn't made available to them until two years after it was launched as an export model; and although it was supremely reliable, at that stage no operator knew this because it was yet untried at home and by this time operators had gone out and bought Scania, Volvo, Mercedes, DAF, etc. That two-year gap appears on the surface to have been ill-conceived: maybe ERF should have marketed it in the UK back in 1973 before it was too late.

Other factors may have included ERF's sparse back-up on the Continent and the fact that the NGC was only available in LHD. Also, the NGC was apparently limited to a road speed of just under 60 mph to suit the lower permissible speeds on the Continent. Reading through the dense technical data in *Commercial Motor*'s catalogue for the 1974 motor show,

(Photo: ERF promo)

I noticed a detail I hadn't come across before: the NGC was 'governed' to 92 kph, which equates to a tad under 60 mph, the UK speed limit for HGVs. Indeed, drivers have confirmed to me that their top speed on the flat was around the 60 mph mark.

This limiting of the NGC's top speed had its roots in the history of early ERF 3MW-cabbed 'Europeans' that were found to be travelling at speeds in excess of 80 mph on Belgian motorways before ERF intervened. Their solution was to fit the direct-top version of the Fuller RT9509A gearbox and raise the axle ratio. Jack Cooke, who designed the NGC, was quoted in *Motor Transport* (20 May 1977) as commenting that, 'This gave us two benefits. We gained about two per cent efficiency changing from the overdrive box. Also, by using a numerically lower ratio axle, further gains were made in mechanical efficiency.' This led to a policy of standardising on direct top gearboxes for all European export models, including the NGC, with suitably higher ratio rear axles.

This might account for the NGC's reliability and longevity on long-haul work, especially as the 335 bhp engine was powerful for its time and had surprisingly high torque at low revs (one of the original 'let it lug' machines). Bearing in mind that NGCs ran on 1200x20 tyres, 1973–75 NGCs had the RT9095A with 4.64:1 final drive ratio; and from 1975–77 they had the RT9509 with 4.71:1 final ratio. In fact, the NGC used in Pat Kennett's 1975 Euro Test had the 4.64:1 final drive, giving a top speed of about 94 kph/59 mph at 2100 rpm: quite respectable for a Continental premium tractor of the period. It is interesting though to note that Pat was reported in the Dutch magazine *Beroepsvervoer* (August 1975) as saying that he was satisfied with the handling and steering of the ERF but thought the overall gearing a little low.

This gearing, instigated to prevent abuse of the driveline abroad, might account for ERF's refusal to supply NGCs to UK operators in the first two years and its refusal to sell a UK-spec version for domestic use. In other words, the NGC was better suited to the lower motorway speeds in Europe and the much lower average speeds on the Middle East run than the M1 on a Friday night! NGCs were doing the Middle

East run at exactly the same time that BBC's *Destination Doha* was being filmed. That film gives a good idea of the kind of terrain encountered after leaving Dover, and of course the gearing begins to make sense.

(Photo: Dave Wallace)

To sum up, it was never really going to be an issue if a Middle East-bound NGC was a bit 'slow' at 59 mph down the M2 to Dover or even if it cost a gallon or two more of diesel because it would actually earn its real keep doing a return long-haul trip, which is exactly what it was designed to do.

This brings us back to the question of why the NGC wasn't offered readily to the domestic market. The answer, in my opinion, is simple. ERF's NGC was supplied with a choice of two NTC engines and two Fuller Road-Ranger gearboxes. It didn't need all sorts of variations: it was built as an export Euro-spec premium tractor. Everything else was covered by other ERF models: 6x4 units, domestic 32-tonners and heavy-haulage tractors were all available as A-series, B-series or MW-cabbed models, along with all their options for alternative gearboxes and engines. The NGC remained to the end a pretty pure beast, it seems; especially as almost all the variations not listed in the sales brochure were retro-fitted by customers who could have chosen one of those alternative models.

(Photo: ERF promo)

IN EUROPE: KING OF THE MOUNTAINS

(Photo: Richard Davies/author's collection)

In *Lorries of Arabia: ERF NGC*, I described why *TRUCK* magazine's editor and truck-tester Pat Kennett had called the NGC 420 'King of the mountains' in his 1975 Euro Test: hence the title of this section. Essentially, the ERF NGC 'European' was pitted against several contemporary Euro-units, including a Scania 140, and the ERF stormed around the gruelling Ardennes route and beat everything in sight. This was put down to a combination of its lively Cummins NTC engine, very slick constant-mesh 9-speed Fuller gearbox and the standard fitment of a Jake Brake. It was registered KDM 460N.

Following the success of the NGC on this Euro-Test, Pat is reported to have said that potentially it was a Euro-beater but they (ERF's management) didn't know how to market or sell it, let alone realise what they had got. He went on to say that ERF was more interested in Cheshire's total industry volume of registrations of new trucks than what the potential was in Belgium, Holland, France and Switzerland.

(Photos: Van Steenbergen archives)

The picture of LHD ERFs in the Van Steenbergen fleet in Arendonk, Belgium, shows how much higher the driver sat in the NGC compared with the B-series. Other similar pictures bear this out. Actually, the whole cab rode higher. Even taking into account the NGC's shallower windscreen, it is clear that its steering wheel is higher and its external sun visor is substantially higher than that of the B-series. Notice too, that the B-series unit's high roof is level with the flat roof of the NGC. The LHD Euro-spec B-series with the full-size sleeper was revealed at Earls Court in September 1976, thus overlapping with production of the NGC for just over a year, the last NGC being dispatched in December 1977. One weekend at Kelsall I drove both an NGC and a B-series around the arena and experienced the difference for myself.

A minor detail: looking at the tread-plate (chequer-plate) on NGC units, it seems that the customer could request this in three places:

On the tow-pack above the bumper for accessing the windscreen
On the recessed door steps
On the door sills

Some units have no plate at all, some have it in one, two, or all three of these locations.

Later models had grab-handles on the top of the front grille to facilitate easy windscreen cleaning. However, in the mid-'70s, when health & safety regulations were not yet the big issues they are today, the importance of foot holds would have paled into insignificance on a lorry like the ERF NGC, into whose cab you had to climb by means of the step-ring on the wheel hub – useless in wet weather – and a few grab handles. I'll bet more than a few NGC drivers suffered from barked shins! This unit was one of six supplied to Van Steenbergen in Arendonk, Belgium and was the original unit exhibited at the Brussels show in January 1973.

Hans Witte's set of drawings of this vehicle appears at the end of this book.

The cutting reminds us that a number of export ERF NGCs went through Cummins Distributor Belgium (CDB), who acted as both importer and dealer. However, it also shows that Van Steenbergen of Arendonk was an ERF dealer. The photo of their premises at the time shows a prominent ERF sign hanging outside the office. Fleet no. 28 languishes below. Van Steenbergen ran six NGCs with Cummins 335s and 9-speed Fullers.

E.R.F. Service in Europe

As more and more E.R.F. trucks operate on the European Continent it becomes vitally important that service back-up can be found wherever a driver's journey happens to take him.

This Section of the Gazetteer lists the E.R.F. Main Distributors in Europe. Every Distributor has fully trained staff who will undertake all manner of repairs and servicing work and has at his disposal a comprehensive stock of genuine E.R.F. replacement parts.

BELGIUM

Cummins Distributor Belgium S.A. — E.R.F. DISTRIBUTOR
623/629 Chaussee de Haecht,
Brussels 3, Belgium.
Telephone 02/168110
Telex 25 177

Garage "De Arend" — E.R.F. DEALER
De Daries, 8, 2370 Arendonk, Belgium
Telephone 014/677042

(From ERF handbook)

(Photo: Van Steenbergen archives)

Hans Witte took this picture at the 1975 motor show in Brussels. He has had a soft spot for NGCs ever since and some of his excellent artwork is shown at the end of this volume.

(Photo: Hans Witte)

Much has been written, both in this series and elsewhere, about the possible shortcomings of ERF's European network's ability to cope with the low volume of trucks involved (compared with larger manufacturers). Contrary to speculation, a piece in *Commercial Motor* during that period indicates that ERF was certainly intent on getting this right. For a start, they had appointed three main distributors in Europe, namely Best Truck Import BV in Holland, Cummins Distributor Belgium SA (CDB) and Societe MABO, who were supported by number of registered repairers throughout France. A Service Gazetteer, listing ERF distributors in the UK and Europe, was made available. The dealers and registered repairers throughout Europe were directly responsible to the main distributor in that particular territory, who in turn were responsible directly to ERF Ltd in the UK.

They also had service representatives / engineers whose job it was to liaise with the European distributors and registered repairers. There was also a procedure to deal with VOR (vehicle off road) repairs and they offered, in conjunction with a private air company, a direct link to any part of Europe should that service be required. In addition, they

(Advert from **Beroepsvervoer** *magazine, 17 September 1975, Holland)*

negotiated with the IRU a credit card scheme so that they could offer this facility to both European and UK operators. This is borne out by a letter to the press from NGC driver Bob Sanders in the Middle East section of this book praising this level of support from ERF.

ERF had a list of all UK operators running ERF vehicles to and from the Continent and offered a service repair facility for any model of ERF vehicle in the form of a 'first aid' repair kit. ERF continually added to their list of outlets throughout Europe and, as their number of vehicles was relatively small, were able to give a first-class service even to areas such as Frankfurt if required.

As reported in the introduction, we now know of no factory built double-drive examples, all known NGCs having been built as 4x2

(Photo: Patrick Battiau)

units. This picture shows that the heavy haulage 6x4 tractive unit operated by Cauvas of Bonneuil-en-France started life as a 4x2 unit. It was either converted to 6x4 or its cab and identity was passed to a donor non-NGC 6x4 chassis. It should be noted that it was not a factory 6x4 as stated in the first book.

The Cauvas unit is seen here with Poclain 1000 excavator going from Flamanville (dept 50) to Paluel (dept 76) on 22 April 1980.

(Photo: Pierre Leboulanger)

(Photo: Private French collection)

In this shot, 8264RW95 is seen in its 6x4 form hauling a 38-metre long refining column weighing 95 tonnes from Moult (dept 14) to Donges in (dept 44) on 27 January 1981.

Here is a picture of JDF 132N as an ERF demonstrator. It was leased by ERF dealer Beech's Garage to Grocott, who used it for Middle East work. It then passed to Beresford Transport of Tunstall and eventually to Trans Arabia.

(Photo: Grocott)

(Photo: Ken Beresford collection)

(Photo: Ken Beresford collection)

JDF 132N is seen again here in this line-up of lorries in the Beresford's rather impressive yellow and two-tone green livery. It was owned by Beresford Transport and based in Le Havre on French number plates for the JCB contract. This contract involved the transport of excavators from Uttoxeter to Southampton, where they were shipped across to Le Havre. The French Beresford driver would then take the trailer the short distance to Philitrans – a company in which Beresford had shares – from where the excavators would be distributed throughout France.

When it was disposed of, the late Vince Cooke picked it up from Stoke and took it to Jones of Aldridge to be prepared for its new life as Trans Arabia 125 out in Jeddah.

This table is from the July 1978 issue of *TRUCK* magazine and gives a fascinating insight into how well the ERF NGC stacked up against its opponents, even after production ceased.

FUEL CONSUMPTION

Truck	Lit/100km	% rating
MAN 19.280	44.94	100
Seddon Atkinson E290	45.18	99.4
Scania LB111.02	45.41	98.9
Daf FT2800DKS	46.28	97.1
Leyland Marathon 2 (TL12)	49.06	91.6
Volvo F12	49.11	91.5
MAN 22.280 (6×2)	49.24	91.2
Magirus Deutz 320M19	49.76	90.3
Fiat 170/35	49.93	90.0
Mercedes Benz 1932	50.16	89.5
MAN 19.320 (V10)	50.18	89.4
ERF 40C2 (B)	50.78	88.4
Ford HA4231	51.07	87.9
Magirus 310D16	51.76	86.8
Bedford TM3800	51.82	86.7
Berliet TR320	51.90	86.4
Volvo F89	52.42	85.7
Ford HA4234	53.55	83.9
Leyland MTC3832	53.80	83.5
ERF NGC420	54.06	83.1
Scania LB140 (V8)	54.41	82.5
Saviem SM340	55.02	81.6

ROUTE SPEED

Truck	kph	% rating
Fiat 170/35	63.63	100
ERF NGC420	62.87	98.8
Leyland Marathon 2 (TL12)	62.18	97.7
Ford HA4234	62.15	97.6
Volvo F12	62.04	97.5
ERF 40C2	61.99	97.4
Scania LB111.02	61.84	97.1
Magirus Deutz 320M19	61.61	96.8
Seddon Atkinson E290	61.61	96.8
Ford HA4231	61.19	96.1
MAN 22.280 (6×2)	60.90	95.7
Bedford TM3800	60.02	95.2
MAN 19.320	60.61	95.1
Mercedes Benz 1932	60.14	94.5
Magirus 310D16	59.68	93.7
Volvo F89	59.46	93.4
Saviem SM340	59.32	93.2
Scania LB140 (V8)	59.19	93.0
MAN 19.280	59.06	92.8
Berliet TR320	57.94	91.0
Leyland MTC3832	57.60	90.5
Daf FT2800DKS	56.65	89.0

PRODUCTIVITY

Truck	% rating
Seddon Atkinson E290	100
Scania LB 111.02	99.805
MAN 19.280	96.446
Fiat 170/35	93.536
Leyland Marathon 2 (TL12)	93.009
Volvo F12	92.718
Magirus Deutz 320M19	90.845
MAN 22.280 (6×2)	90.708
Daf FT2800DKS	89.814
ERF 40C2	89.485
MAN 19.320 (V10)	88.360
Mercedes Benz 1932	87.808
Ford HA4231	87.780
Bedford TM3800	85.782
ERF NGC420	85.329
Ford HA4234	85.029
Magirus 310D16	84.431
Volvo F89	83.133
Berliet TR320	81.636
Scania LB140	79.640
Saviem SM340	78.942
Leyland MTC3832	78.443

The tables show fuel consumption, road speeds and productivity ratings of the 22 trucks that have been tested in this series over the past four years. It should be remembered that most of the trucks near the bottom of the productivity table have now been superseded or are about to be superseded.

67

(From TRUCK *magazine)*

One of the paradoxes of our time is that all modern sleeper-cabbed tractive units are fit for long-haul work to pretty well anywhere, but in the UK we rarely send them further than our shores. Forty years ago, the combination of our entry into the Common Market and the Middle East boom meant that we had to realise a new concept: off-the-peg British 4x2 forward-control premium long-haul LHD Euro-spec tractive units with sleeper cabs and respectable drive-lines. Among these were the Seddon 39:Four with its Rolls Royce 280 + 9-speed Fuller; the Seddon-Atkinson 400 with its Cummins 335 + 9-speed Fuller; the Bedford TM with its Cummins 290 or Detroit 400 + 9-speed Fuller; the Ford Transcontinental with its Cummins 290 or 335 + 9-speed Fuller; the Leyland Marathon with its TL12 or Cummins 335 + 9-speed Fuller; the ERF MGC with its Cummins 335 + 9-speed Fuller; the ERF B-series with its Cummins 290 and 9-speed Fuller; and, of course, the ERF NGC 'European' with its Cummins 335 + 9-speed Fuller. Some of these had 13-speed Fuller options but that's a detail. The point is, we had to manufacture premium long-haulers to compete with the Continentals. The NGC, in my humble opinion was the best contender.

(Photo: ERF promo)

This picture was taken at the Brussels 1973 motor show. We know from the archives that the first NGC to be dispatched in March 1973 was AFU 615 (fleet no. 28) in the Belgian fleet, Van Steenbergen of Arendonk. To

(Photo: Adrian Cypher)

the left is the draw-bar outfit that went to another Belgian fleet, Ets Thibaut of Stree. It was the second NGC dispatched from Sandbach.

This breakdown wagon is seen here on trade plates in the livery of Reliable Recovery Services, rescuing a Ford Transcontinental in Dover. It had also been operated by BFI Recovery services. Registered Q824 RGC it may have been a pre-production NGC draw-bar outfit. This theory is supported by the absence of a roof vent, the absence of roof-mounted side-lights and the addition of a non-standard, grille-top water inspection lid. Furthermore, it has the same design of backing for the ERF letters as the prototype, with broad lateral slats instead of narrow ones. These are all features that distinguish the prototype tractive unit. Its external sun visor appears to be from a B-series unit.

Interestingly, there was an NGC with a modified roof vent – probably to comply with petroleum regulations. Registered HMO 220N, it was operated by Estra BV in Rotterdam on sub-contract to Calor Transport. The driver of the Estra/Calor unit was able to confirm that HMO 220N was the only NGC they had. This got me thinking about other channel-hopping NGCs operated by UK hauliers. For some reason, Estra registered their NGC in the UK even though it was based in Holland. However, this was not always the case. Long before 'flagging out' became popular (i.e. registering a lorry abroad on foreign plates whilst still operating from a base in the UK), certain UK operators established bases in French Channel ports and operated their French-registered units from there. These units were used for the Continental leg of international journeys and usually entailed dropping trailers off at French Channel ports for unaccompanied shipment to UK Channel ports. Two examples that spring immediately to mind are Beresford's NGC based in Le Havre and EH Nicholls's two LHD E-series ERFs based in Calais. Very few people on this side of the Channel would have been aware of the vehicles involved in this kind of operation because they would never see those units at work. One wonders, then, if more NGCs fell into this category.

(Photo: Gerdi Kimpe)

Bertrand Guwez operated BER 329 on heavy haulage in Brugge (Bruges), Belgium. It is pictured with its driver in Book 2. This NGC was eventually replaced by a B-series ERF. Tempting though it is to blame ERF's limited Continental export success on the need for imperial, rather than metric, tooling for maintenance; it should be remembered that American hardware was very popular at that time, especially in France and the Low Countries. Also, workshops on both sides of the Channel were generally equipped for both.

MMG 772P is a good example of the ten or so NGCs used by UK companies for Channel-hopping duties to Europe rather than for long-haul work. It was operated by A.J. Bradick of Leyton until G.L. Baker acquired them along with some of the vehicles including this ERF NGC. It worked out of G.L. Baker's Faversham depot running to Paris, after which it was used by their Silvertown depot on a NYK containers contract. The regular driver of MMG 772P claimed that it gave the Scania 140s a run for their money – a sentiment of which Pat Kennett would have approved (given the '75 Euro-Test!)

(Photo: Dean Bartlett collection)

This unit seems to have wound up as a shunter with a company making concrete railway sleepers. It had a Cummins 335 and 9-speed Fuller. A second NGC is believed to have been used on the NYK contract and it was painted in the livery of Van Ommeren.

(Photo: Nigel Bunt)

(Photo: Ted Croswell)

KRH 153P was one of the UK NGCs operated by Phil Horridge of Poole on Spain and Portugal work and is described in the previous two volumes in this series. The first picture shows it in Horridge colours pulling the kind of 12-metre step-frame tilt often associated with groupage work.

However, new intelligence has come to light. Firstly, that Phil acquired it from Ted Croswell of Hull, who ran it in the earlier livery shown in this picture: white cab with a broad red waistband and a red and white bumper, plus two air horns and an Australian-style windscreen stone guard. Secondly, and surprisingly, that apparently it was originally

(Photo: ERF promo)

fitted with a Cummins 250 – one of only two NGCs thought to be thus equipped. This might explain why it later acquired a Cummins 350 from a heavy plant machine!

This NGC was exhibited alongside the B-series at the 1974 Amsterdam show, by the Dutch importer Best Truck Imports of Oud Beijerland near Rotterdam. The NGC entered service with Groen of Nieuw Lekkerland as 16-37-FB.

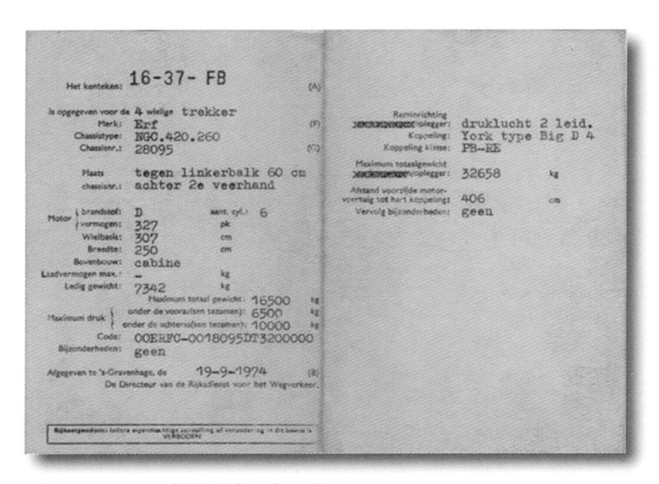

Het kenteken: 16-37- FB (A)

is opgegeven voor de 4 wielige trekker
Merk: Erf (F)
Chassistype: NGC.420.260
Chassisnr.: 28095 (C)

Plaats chassisnr.: tegen linkerbalk 60 cm achter 2e veerhand

Motor brandstof: D aant. cyl.: 6
vermogen: 327 pk
Wielbasis: 307 cm
Breedte: 250 cm
Bovenbouw: cabine
Laadvermogen max.: – kg
Ledig gewicht: 7342 kg
Maximum totaal gewicht: 16500 kg
Maximum druk onder de vooras(sen tezamen): 6500 kg
onder de achteras(sen tezamen): 10000 kg
Code: 00ERFC-0018095DT3200000
Bijzonderheden: geen

Afgegeven te 's-Gravenhage, de 19-9-1974 (B)
De Directeur van de Rijksdienst voor het Wegverkeer.

Reminrichting oplegger: druklucht 2 leid.
Koppeling: York type Big D 4
Koppeling klasse: PB-HE

Maximum totaalgewicht oplegger: 32658 kg

Afstand voorzijde motorvoertuig tot hart koppeling: 406 cm
Vervolg bijzonderheden: geen

(From original ERF log book)

The second image shows the original log book. Its date of registration in Holland is given as 19 September 1974 and the unit weighs in at a fairly heavy 7342 kg. The chassis number is shown as 28095, which is valuable evidence as we have very few chassis numbers for NGCs.

Apparently, the B-series on display went to Prooi of Barendrecht. Those pre-September 1976 LHD B-series were just replacements for the domestic A-series 32-tonner and were supplied with Cummins 250 engines. It is thought that Prooi may also have run an NGC.

With regard to Best Truck Imports, there were at least two Bestebreurtje brothers; P. Bestebreurtje operating from Rijsoord and W.T. Bestebreurtje in Oud-Beijerland. They worked together in the '50s and '60s. Then in the '70s they became Auto Bestebreurtje BV (DAF dealer), Rijksstraatweg 219, Rijsoord; and Best Trucks Import BV (ERF importers), Rembrandtstraat 4, Oud-Beijerland. Later, in about 1984, they closed and formed a new company called Best Trucks. They moved to Barendrecht and opened three more workshops in Dordrecht, Europoort and Oude-Tonge.

(Photo: ERF promo)

The NGC operated by Barend Sjouw of Poortugaal, pulling Van Uden trailers in Rotterdam is pictured above. It was exhibited at the 1976 Amsterdam motor show. Note that it still has its Dutch pre-registration plate N-06-55 before it was issued with its proper registration number, 41-54-NB. It had the combination of Cummins NTC 335 and 9-speed Fuller. The standard fitment was a Fuller RT9509 or RT9509A (slightly different ratios), both of which had an H-pattern gate with an H-pattern shift. By the way, the 13-speed Fuller offered with the NTC 290 could be an RT9513 or the U-shift pattern RTO9513 overdrive version.

It was reported in Book 1 that Barend Sjouw traded his NGC in for a B-series after just one year because he wanted a better fuel return. Also reported was the information that Dutch operators preferred the more frugal B-series, even if the drivers didn't. However, it is important to recognise that many of the LHD B-series sold in Holland were for domestic use in a flat landscape and that these vehicles were ERF sleeper conversions with the Cummins NHC 250 engine (an older, naturally aspirated version of the same 14-litre lump) – hardly a comparable unit with the powerful longer-haul NGC. Barend Sjouw's replacement B-series was one such vehicle. Therefore, it seems prudent not to attach significance to the fuel factor in the NGC's demise. In any case, as reported elsewhere in this volume, ERF was already experimenting with the big-cam 290 in the NGC, which would have put it on a par with the later high-roof Euro-spec B-series that had the same engine.

This NGC is a bit of a mystery. It is photographed here in Italy with what looks like Comart colours pulling an MJL tilt (Michael John Luff). Older Comart drivers report having seen such a unit in their colours. A recent contributor leads me to believe that it was French-registered and briefly operated by LTL (Luff Transport Ltd), after which it was sold on to a small Belgian operator as it was a non-standard unit. The NGC was type-approved in France

(Photo: Pasquale Caccavale)

(ERF adverts)

at 42 tonnes gcw. Little is known about this French unit, registered 7681RR91, but you can sense that early morning autumn chill in the air, the prospect of demisting the windscreen and the choking, acrid fumes from the big engine when you initially started it up for a day's work in those days. Another picture I have shows it with a flatbed trailer, so we can only guess what work it undertook.

(Photo: Alberto Pesanti, Italy)

I have a theory about the fate of this unit. A French contributor – a former heavy haulage driver himself – reported that this photo was taken on the premises of Cauvas in Bonneuil en France, where it stood for some time to be used for spare parts. As reported elsewhere in this volume, we know that Cauvas already had an NGC registered 8264RW95 that they converted from 4x2 to 6x4, possibly using a Volvo bogie. Also reported, this time by a Dutch contributor, was that a LHD ERF MCC with a 3MW cab belonging to Hye of Antwerp in Belgium passed into the hands of Cauvas after being damaged in a road accident and subsequently received a 7MW cab. It is possible that the pictured NGC was the donor vehicle for this cab. For the purposes of our quest for the 91 NGCs, however, it is academic whether or not the Cauvas cab ended up with a Volvo rear end or ended up atop an ERF MCC 852: the fact is that only one 4x2 NGC appeared to be involved and we have a registration number and a photo to prove it.

This 1975 unit was operated by Vermeulen of Nieuwerkerk a.d. Ijssel in Holland. It was registered 05-17-FB and had a Cummins NTC 335 engine. Here is a price list from the Dutch importer and dealer of ERFs for 1975. The cost of the basic spec translates into about £16,788.

(Photo: Leo Mes)

BEST TRUCK

Price list (4 August 1975)

NGC 420 series 270 – 335 SAE hp	
Tractor 4 x 2	*f* 95.000,00
Truck 4 x 2	*f* 92.500,00

Basic spec:

Sleeper cab with curtains and one bed, sprayed in your colour, two Viking Bostrom seats, co-drivers' seat with head- and armrests, radio-cassette player, fire extinguisher, coco mats, 2- line + 24 V including curling-hoses, automatic cooler fan, Jacobs engine brake, York Big D coupling, rear mudguards, tow hook in front bumper, and Luberfiner oil filter which enables an oil-change every 20,000 km.

Optionals at extra costs:

Central lubrication device	from *f* 2.000,00
Air dryer instead of anti-frost pot	750,00
Electric connection 12 = 24 V	175,00
Second bed	450,00
12.00 x 20 Michelin x 18 P.R.	950,00
Michelin XZA at front axle	250,00
Air horn	250,00
Toolbox	from 250,00
Sun visor transparent	350,00
Laminated front screen	500,00
ML tectyl treatment	300,00

Hazardous Transport equipment: price at request.
All prices above are excluded VAT.

COMPARISON

Prices in Holland in August 1975 for comparable 4x2 tractors with two-bed sleeper cab. Prices are theoretical, in practice the real prices were negotiated.

ERF NGC	*f* 95.450,00
DAF FT2800 DKS	95.750,00
Mercedes-Benz 1932 S (long sleeper cab)	102.950,00
Saviem SM340	90.500,00
Scania LB 140 S	101.650,00
Volvo F89	107.185,00

Information supplied by Hans Witte.

Loste of Lille, in France, was a serious heavy haulage specialist. It had two of these NGCs. Oddly, it also had a Pacific with the same cab – seemingly a retro-fitted 7MW (or possibly 8MW) – that later passed

(Photo: Raoul)

on to another heavy haulage firm in Lille called Sitca. Details of these vehicles can be found in the NGC register at the back of this book.

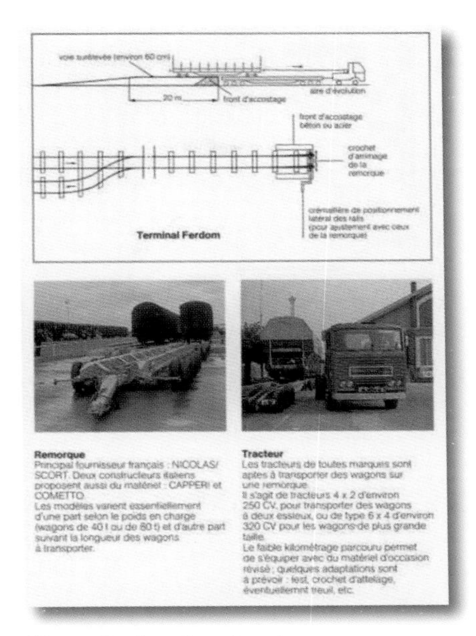

voie surélevée (environ 60 cm)
20 m
front d'accostage
aire d'évolution
front d'accostage béton ou acier
crochet d'arrimage de la remorque
crémaillère de positionnement latéral des rails (pour ajustement avec ceux de la remorque)

Terminal Ferdom

Remorque
Principal fournisseur français : NICOLAS/SCORT. Deux constructeurs italiens proposent aussi du matériel : CAPPERI et COMETTO.
Les modèles varient essentiellement d'une part selon le poids en charge (wagons de 40 t ou de 80 t) et d'autre part suivant la longueur des wagons à transporter.

Tracteur
Les tracteurs de toutes marques sont aptes à transporter des wagons sur une remorque.
Il s'agit de tracteurs 4 x 2 d'environ 250 CV, pour transporter des wagons à deux essieux, ou de type 6 x 4 d'environ 320 CV pour les wagons de plus grande taille.
Le faible kilométrage parcouru permet de s'équiper avec du matériel d'occasion révisé ; quelques adaptations sont à prévoir : lest, crochet d'attelage, éventuellemnt treuil, etc.

(From Ferdom brochure)

In my quest to discover all 91 NGCs, some of the later discoveries proved quite elusive. This French example, registered 7583PP89, probably spent its life off the main highways. It was employed as a ballasted tractor on a special system designed by Ferdom to haul railway wagons from the railhead at Sens directly to warehouses by road within the transport hub to be loaded by forklift truck. The wagons were pushed onto a multi-wheeled trailer, into which a railway line was set. From the caption given in Ferdom's brochure it would appear that this particular NGC was fitted with the NHC 250 naturally-aspirated version of the 14-litre Cummins engine used in other NGCs (290 and 335). This engine was offered as an option in the NGC brochures of the '70s.

At the time of writing Part 2, this NGC languishing in France was still awaiting a purchaser and restorer. It was operated by R. Collin Exploitation Foresterie of 89 Montillet.

Many NGCs were supplied with 'west coast' mirrors, as were many A-series of the period, but they were not popular with every driver.

Lorry technology is in a constant state of evolution. Models come and go. Their ephemerality is faintly reminiscent of the life cycle of butterflies, which are continually and minutely evolving in response to the changing world. The NGC might echo one of those epic migratory butterflies as it still represents ERF as the one model conceived for long journeys overseas and for crossing wild frontiers. Both marque and

(*Photos: Phillipe Methurin*)

model have passed in the twinkling of an eye, but we remain vigilant for the odd specimen that may be hibernating in the dusty corner of a barn somewhere …

06-09-TB was supplied to Groenenboom of Ridderkerk in Holland during 1977. The Dutch used to have a pre-registration number system to get the operator up and running with his lorry while the paperwork was being finalised. Groenenboom had two NGCs. One was registered 12-97-FB and had the pre-registration N-11-20 and the other was registered 06-09-TB and had the pre-registration number N-11-48. Hans Witte has drawn a diagram of this truck, which appears in the last section of this book.

The programme below, supplied by Hans Witte, shows the planning of Holland's ERF importer and dealer during the NGC period. It firmly reflects ERF's pulling out of the Continental market in 1979, not to return until after the European borders 'melted' in 1992.

(ERF advert)

(Photo: **Bedrijftransport** *magazine)*

ERF TRUCKS IN HOLLAND

1974–80

Best Trucks Import, Oud-Beijerland

1974

Best Trucks Import starts import of ERF NGC 'European'.
October 1974: first press introduction in *Auto & Transportwereld* and test drive in *Bedrijfsvervoer*.
First advertisement found in *Auto & Transportwereld*, 1 November 1974.

1975

Rai specs in *Bedrijfsvervoer* and *Beroepsvervoer* (February):

NGC 420 tractor 4x2	Cummins NTC 335	*f* 87.500,00
NGC 420 truck 4x2	Cummins NTC 335	90.000,00

Optional: Cummins NTC 290 + Fuller 13 speed.

A multi-truck test was held in May 1975 in cooperation with Truck (Pat Kennett) and published in *Beroepsvervoer* in August 1975. A test with a Groenenboom tractor was published in *Bedrijfsvervoer* in September 1975.

Late 1975: start import ERF B-series.

40C2 TR tractor 4x2	Cummins 250 hp	Fuller 9	75.000,00	B-series
40C2 TR tractor 4x2	Cummins 290 hp	Fuller 13	85.000,00	
Trucks/longer wheel base:			+2.500,00	

Day cab only.

1976

February 1976: introduction of ERF B-series to the public at the RAI exhibition.

NGC 420 tractor 4x2	Cummins NTC 335 328 hp	Fuller 9	87.500,00	European
NGC 420 truck 4x2	Cummins NTC 335 328 hp	Fuller 9	85.000,00	European
40C2 TR tractor 4x2	Cummins NH 250 239 hp	Fuller 9	--	B-series
45 C3 TR tractor 6x4	Cummins NTC 350 334 hp	Fuller 9	--	B-series

Cummins NTC 290 + Fuller 13 speed optional for NGC.
Cummins NTC 290E + Fuller 13 speed optional for 40 C2TR — B-series
Sleeper cab (Jennings) optional for B-series.

1977

Programme unchanged.

(Photo: **Bedrijftransport** *magazine)*

Jan Bestebreurtje of ERF's importer and dealer, Best Trucks, provided this Groenenboom 335-powered unit for *Bedrijftransport* magazine in Holland to test. Their December 1974 issue carried the full report. *Bedrijftransport*'s overall impression was very positive. They found the NGC pleasant to drive in the hills. The tester commented that the constant-mesh 9-speed Fuller installation was made very slick by the Lipe-Rolaway clutch and clutch-brake, all of which was echoed strongly in Pat Kennett's Belgian Euro Test for *TRUCK* magazine six months later. The satisfying driving position and well set up power

(Photo: Rene Postma)

(Photo: Robert Hackford)

steering were also favourably commented upon, as was the standard provision of a Jake Brake. An interesting remark not usually seen in UK tests was that it took 52 secs to accelerate from 50 kph to 80 kph at 41.5 tonnes; which the tester claimed put the NGC among the more flexible trucks of the day.

Rene Postma took this picture after rescuing the Marcel Eyckmans ERF NGC 'European' in Belgium. He transported it with his Volvo F89 to Holland, where restoration was started. The load on the tail end includes two spare cab doors from a Van Steenbergen NGC and two more spare doors sourced from a scrap yard near Betekom. However, Rene sold it on and it was eventually completed by the Corbishleys in England, where it was re-registered as KCH 95N, its Belgian plate having been 7DF44. The full story of this rescue appears in *REVS International* magazine no. 87, written by Wobbe Reitsma.

Here is KCH 95N fully restored, out for a run in the Staffordshire countryside in 2013. It was a remarkably comfortable journey for a lorry of its time. Artwork by Hans Witte showing this unit in its original guise as a tractive unit on timber work in Belgium appears at the end of this book.

ERF NGCs were variously registered in the following countries to my knowledge: Great Britain, Holland, France, Belgium, Switzerland, Saudi Arabia, Kuwait and UAE.

I wonder how many regular drivers an average ERF NGC hosted during its life. We know that there were 91 NGCs built. I have been in contact with a dozen or so drivers but if there are more out there, we'd like to hear from them!

(Photo: Alan Rickett)

ERF, SAND & STARS: MIDDLE EAST

(Photo: David Pilcher)

Well over a third of known NGCs worked in the Middle East, either on 'internals' or as 'overlanders' (see lists at the back of this book). Evidence of yet another NGC on the Middle East run can be seen here in the form of a Swiss owner–driver's unit with a legend in Arabic script on its bumper.

As reported in Book 1, Hans Burkhard of Zurich operated a fully sign-written NGC (ZH 120 919) driven by an Englishman named Harry, who complained about its reliability and hinted at poor maintenance. Hans operated a second NGC that he took on the Middle East run until eventually he was accused of alcohol smuggling and had to abandon his tilt trailer in Saudi. After that his local driver, Marcel Roth, did Germany and Italy with the NGC. This included a contract to import new Schmitz trailers from Altenberge. One of the NGCs was eventually cannibalized for its running gear, which was installed in a Henschel F191 draw-bar outfit. Apparently, this wasn't a success.

There were two more Swiss NGCs in addition to the two operated by H. Burkard. These were both owned by M Knöpfli AG of Regensdorf. This is an engineering company that specializes in transmissions for heavy plant, power stations and marine engines.

One was sold in the late '80s to an owner–driver operating as Zimmermann transport, who wrote it off in Poland. Apparently, this outfit was awarded the NGC by the courts in lieu of unpaid invoices from a haulier called Ohnemus. This possibility, however remote, gives us hope! The other NGC went to a collector who died, so the ERF was sold. Mr Knopfli rather suspects that the vehicle could exist somewhere in the area of Kloten.

The ERF importer and distributor for Switzerland was ERFIM AG of Neuhofstrassen 11, 4153 Reinach/Basel.

Chris Till drove Eric Vick's KFH 249P on Middle East work for five years and reports that it never broke down. It is seen here on the site in Baghdad to which successive VIJORE group ERFs transported the wherewithal to build an entire animal feed mill in the mid-'70s. *Lorries*

(Photo: Chris Till)

of Arabia 2 features a number of excellent pictures and anecdotes from this knowledgeable and experienced driver. I had the pleasure of introducing him to Gary Corbishley's preserved NGC (KCH 95N) at Gaydon Retro Show. Sitting in the driver's seat brought back memories for him.

This picture would have been taken immediately before or after the first trip down to Baghdad with equipment for the construction of the animal feed mill. Kysor roof-mounted air-conditioning units were fitted for subsequent trips. Cummins NTC 335s with 9-speed Fullers were standard equipment on the ERF NGC model.

(Photo: Origin unknown)

Eric Vick, Richard Read and Tony Jones formed a consortium to undertake Middle East duties, initially on a Baghdad contract. They called it VIJORE, using their joint initials. The VIJORE units were painted in a red, white and blue livery, and there were liveried semi-trailers. The odd thing is that only Tony Jones's units seem to have been painted in VIJORE livery. Eric Vick's and Richard Read's units did the work in their own liveries. A range of units were placed on this work, but there were only six ERF NGCs: two in each livery. The two VIJORE-liveried NGCs belonging to Tony Jones eventually passed to Richard Read (NFH 120P and PDF 444R). As VIJORE was set up alongside these three domestic companies, it

(Photo: Mark Bailey)

seems strange that they didn't give the entire set of available vehicles a uniform livery. Perhaps they preferred to switch domestic units in and out of the pool depending on demand (witness the day-cabbed Seddon!).

Poetry in motion: a rare and glorious picture of an NGC out on the open road. It appears to be Richard Read's KFH 250P on post-Middle East duties hauling steel out of Monmouthshire and demonstrating its legendary prowess on the long steep banks.

NFH 120P is seen here in Richard Read livery, though it started life in the livery of VIJORE on Middle East work, as evidenced by the second photograph. It was the only one of the six VIJORE group NGCs to have an NTC 290 engine with a 13-speed Fuller rather than an NTC 335 with a 9-speed Fuller. As well as Baghdad, it did at least one trip to Jeddah.

(Photo: Marcus Lester)

(Photo: Peter Smith)

(Photo: William Mills)

(Photo: Chris Till)

Conditions were often very harsh in winter, especially in Turkey. Here, KFH 249P waits in line showing every sign of having travelled through appalling weather. KFH 250P or 251P in Richard Read livery can be seen behind it. Because of the warm fuel return system in a Cummins engine, these NGCs didn't suffer from waxed fuel whilst running in very cold weather.

Eric Vick had their NTC 335 engines down-rated a bit to improve fuel consumption, which is surprising, given that they carried belly tanks under the trailers to load up with dirt cheap fuel in the Middle East. Nonetheless, this might go a little way towards explaining why both these units were so reliable! Chris Till, who verified this information for me, said, 'Don't be fooled by that news: these NGCs pulled like trains. One day when it was freezing in Turkey the Mercedes (artic) wouldn't start because the filter and fuel lines had waxed up. We put a bar on the front of the Mercedes and onto the back of my trailer and I towed him over the mountains, and I am not kidding you, nothing could overtake us. It was only when we stopped that Neil told me he was freezing cold so he had put the Mercedes into gear to turn the engine over to give him some warm from the heater. How's that for pulling power?'

(*Photo: Chris Till*)

Eric Vick and Richard Read ERF NGCs take a break in a lay-by on the way to the Middle East. ERF NGCs went to many of the outposts of what I like to call the 'Wholly Lorriable Empire', including Pakistan. However, I can find no evidence of them having ventured into Russia or North Africa. The reason for Eric Vick not sending NGCs to North Africa was simple: the regular loads were at maximum gross weight and the NGCs were too heavy, so they used B-series ERFs instead!

KFH 249P is pictured with a container at Kingfisher Warf in Bedford. So was the NGC an 'iconic' long-hauler? In recording the historically

(*Photo: Mike Tebbutt*)

acclaimed success of a model whose good reputation quickly faded with the mists of recent time, we may run the risk of romanticizing it by setting it up to be another supposed 'icon' of the '70s Middle East Run. The NGC's noble history speaks for itself.

It was an excellent lorry of its time, regardless of its small production run, and it may or may not deserve a better place in history. Personally, I believe that the notion of long-haul 'icons' is without substance. Instead, there were long-haul *preferences*. The Scania 140 was just as good as the ERF NGC but for different reasons. Discerning drivers may have preferred Scania's V8 engine over ERF's straight-six Cummins – they were both 14-litre. Or they may have preferred ERF's 9-speed Fuller constant-mesh gearbox over Scania's 10-speed synchromesh one. It is rare to find a group of seasoned drivers who will agree upon the 'best'.

In the first couple of pictures VIJORE's PDF 444R is parked somewhere in the desert. This was one of the later NGCs and had a Cummins 335 with 9-speed Fuller. Noted for its trip to Karachi in Pakistan in my earlier books, this 4x2 unit was later acquired by Tony Kimber, who ran Shamara, a heavy haulage outfit in Southampton. At first it ran on container work but was then converted to 6x4. Q-plates were issued for rebuilds (including cut-and-shut conversions) as well as second-hand imports and vehicles of indeterminate age, so it was re-registered Q691 NTR and formed part of a push–pull combination with a rare Scammell Samson (registered Q362 NTR) to move a girder trailer loaded with

(Photo: Origin unknown)

(Photo: Stephen John Heward)

(Photos: Ady Goodman)

Pirelli reels. It then passed to Raynor Plant in Alfreton, Derbyshire – as seen in the third picture here – and it finally finished up in a breaker's yard, that of Roger Geesons, Hammersmith, Ripley, as shown in the fourth picture. The other NGC to receive a Q-plate was Q824 RGC, which was converted from a 4x2 tractive unit to a recovery wagon.

KFH 248P is seen here in a side street near the Opera Hotel and the British Club in Baghdad. Its regular driver was John Matley, but it was also driven by David Cleat. In the British Club drivers could enjoy good food by the pool.

(Photo: Bjorn Kjer)

Another erstwhile driver of NGCs with Eric Vick was Bob Sanders. He wrote a letter to *TRUCK* magazine in 1985 stoutly defending the use of ERFs on long-haul work. 'One would find it extremely difficult to find a more reliable and economical truck,' he claimed; and went on to say, 'Whenever any spares have been required abroad ERF put them on the first available aircraft so you were never at a standstill for long.'

Eric Vick ran these two tank containers from the UK to Istanbul on three round trips, refilling with aerosol propellant in Rotterdam. The NGC in the photo is KFH 249P, driven at that time by the late Roger Williams.

(Photo: Chris Jeffries)

Chris Till himself appears in this picture in front of KFH 249P. He said, 'It was a fantastic lorry: it just pulled and pulled like a train and was utterly reliable.'

(Photo: Chris Till)

The Kysor air-con and breather pipes can be clearly seen in this Middle East shot. You can almost smell the cardamom coffee and hear the Arabic popular music spilling from neighbouring terraces.

For me, this magnificent black and white image is a classic: take a walk in a paradise garden in mid-summer and stumble upon the ultimate long-haul tractive unit of the period!

(Photo: Paul Gee)

ERF had designed the roof hatch to accommodate a Kysor air-conditioning unit. Thus burdened with an air-con unit, the roof structure transpired to be unequal to the stresses and strains of Middle East roads so Trans Arabia installed a form of Acro-prop within the cab to stop the ceiling from sagging.

It is quite clear that the VIJORE group were onto this case, too. Later pictures of the Eric Vick and Richard Read NGCs with air-con show stout rails mounted on the roof to distribute the weight of the air-con units, as seen here.

These two photos show the same unit in its early days. In the second shot, the breather pipes can be clearly seen and appear to be

(Photos: Paul Gee)

chassis-mounted. They were later braced to the rear of the cab and tilted with it.

(Photo: Chris Till)

This line-up of Middle East-bound lorries includes both of Eric Vick's NGCs along with a Ford Transcontinental that also belonged to them, and a day-cabbed Seddon – brave driver!

Because its main heavy truck output consisted of standard domestic day-cabbed 32-tonne artics, ERF probably wasn't at the forefront of the minds of hauliers buying long-haul tractive units. Perhaps it wasn't so much a question of whether the NGC was inferior, but more of a question of whether operators chose unwisely. It should be remembered and acknowledged that the NGC was certainly fit for purpose in its day and was arguably every bit as good as the competition.

(Photo: Eric Vick archives)

This image shows the newly delivered pair of NGCs on Eric Vick's premises in 1975. An older A-series ERF can be seen, too. KFH 248P and KFH 249P made a trip to Baghdad before the roof-mounted air-conditioner units were fitted.

In 1981, Bandag claimed that using its procure retread tyres on a typical transcontinental artic such as Eric Vick's NGCs, a 'thumping' £64 saving could be made on a 4280-mile Gloucester–Istanbul round trip. This was projected to give Vick an annual saving of £750 on just one truck, assuming a mileage of 50,000. An advertisement to this effect, complete with a picture of one of Eric Vick's NGCs, appears in Book 2.

JLG 35N was an ERF demonstrator. It was fully equipped for the Middle East run, complete with Kysor air-con, visor and breather pipes, and was sent out there on tour along with its trailer, which was also a demonstrator. The photographer, a former publicity officer for ERF, informed me that in the days of the NGCs, demo units were fitted with the biggest engines, so it's reasonable to assume that NGC demonstrators had Cummins NTC 335s with 9-speed Fuller 'boxes.

I met Bill Fitzsimons, who worked for ERF as a field engineer and was occasionally flown out to the Middle East. It was he who drove JLG 35N on its Middle East tour. He shipped into Beirut. According to *Commercial Motor* (11 July 1975), foreign lorries could cross Lebanon if they were empty. Bill then crossed Lebanon, Syria, Jordan and Saudi Arabia (down the TAP-line) to enter Qatar. Before Doha, he encountered an atrocious sandstorm that not only obliterated the road, but it frosted his headlamp lenses and buffed the paintwork. Finally, Bill drove it to Kuwait, where it was sold. He remembers the trip with great fondness, having enjoyed driving the NGC. Bill spoke very highly indeed of this model and believes many more could have been sold with different marketing. One other demo vehicle accompanied him on this trip: JLB 34N, an ERF dump truck.

(Photo: Alan Rickett)

Having been in communication with both ERF's field engineer who drove it and their publicity officer who photographed it in Sandbach, I rather hoped to unearth a rich hoard of images from this trip but none has come to light and perhaps they were lost. Tempting though it is to wonder if the golden opportunity to take legion promotional pictures of their flagship unit in such photogenic surroundings was simply missed by ERF, it does well to remember that many happy snappers – including the photo-journalists who rode shotgun on the Middle East run to write *Cola Cowboys* and *Juggernaut* – lost all their photographs to the Saudi security apparatus.

(Photos: Mick Jones)

(Photo: Robert Hackford)

These three pictures show number 126 in the Trans Arabia fleet in Jeddah. Trans Arabia operated on 'internals' out of Jeddah in Saudi Arabia as an offshoot of S. Jones of Aldridge in partnership with Bin Zagr. In the second picture it can be seen on 'road-train' duties, which was commonplace for Trans Arabia in those days. The third picture shows its original Dutch registration plate. 84-56-JB was supplied to Ben Schaap of Rotterdam in 1976 and was the first ERF with ADR status in Holland. When some years later S. Jones bought it second-hand and prepared it for its new life as no. 126 in the Trans Arabia fleet in Jeddah, the plate was replaced with a Saudi one, but never thrown away! It proved vital in providing conclusive evidence that they were one and the same vehicle. It is now a memento.

In such arduous conditions accidents were almost inevitable. This Trans Arabia ERF NGC was eventually righted and continued to work. They often ran across the desert at high weights with a second artic trailer behind, and are reported to have performed superbly and been extremely reliable. Incidentally, John Davies who took the photo was a mechanic for Trans Arabia and had actually worked on the NGC production line at ERF.

(Photo: John Davies)

(Photo: John Davies)

Sometimes one of Trans Arabia's NGCs would be loaded with packing cases and reels of cable for Racal Communications. According to the erstwhile TA director, Ken Broster, loads such as this were overseen and guided by Racal's ex-SAS man. These were security-sensitive loads for the Ministry of the Interior and were taken to extremely remote corners of the Saudi kingdom. Apparently, TA did quite a few of these special consignments. The driver would pick up the guide and off they'd go. It was a good earner!

(Photo: Jerry Cooke)

Trans Arabia operated out of Jeddah in Saudi Arabia. I didn't work for them, of course, but I did drive lorries overland to the Arabian Gulf and North Africa; and it seems to me that the work those lads did on 'internals' was a different game entirely. Those who drove, repaired, maintained, operated, managed and purchased for this outfit were a pretty amazing and resilient lot, and their tales are often enthralling!

(Photo: John Davies)

The retelling of this segment of trucking history in these volumes is a celebration of British grit in the Arabian deserts; a celebration of S. Jones's brave Middle East venture; a celebration of the true potential of the ERF's mighty NGCs; and a celebration of Trans Arabia's part in the great history of the TIR trail.

Trans Arabia 109 is seen here with one of its regular drivers, Manni Gobani, when it was based in Dammam. Jerry Cooke reports that Manni was a 'really good driver' and he remembers towing Manni from Turaif 800 miles down the TAP-line to Dammam on a straight bar attached to the back of a 40-ft trailer when the ERF had broken down.

Another of its regular drivers was Dave Anslow but another driver, Dennis Purchase, once took it on a rare international trip to Kuwait. The general manager, Ken Broster, pointed out to me that discolouring below the headlights evident in the picture of 109 in Book 1 was a result

(Photo: Jerry Cooke)

of the sand-blasting effect resulting from driving into sandstorms. Apparently, this was a common occurrence. Ken inherited the NGCs when he took over and was instrumental in ordering the Macks. Although he thought highly of the NGCs and their ability to work in arduous conditions, he thought that 6x4s, not 4x2s, should have been spec'd because of the terrain and the high weights carried.

(Photo: John Davies)

In 1977, 12-97-FB finished its life with Groenenboom of Ridderkirk in Holland and was sold to another Dutchman called Steef Slappendel, who used it on the Middle East run. It ended up in Jeddah, Saudi Arabia, where Trans Arabia acquired it and sent it back to Aldridge to be

(Photo: Alan Ball)

overhauled and repainted bearing the fleet number 139. It is shown in this picture loaded on a trailer ready to be sent back out to Jeddah.

Motor Transport of 7 July 1978 gave a thorough account of Cunard's subsidiary, Cunard Arabian Middle East Line (CAMEL), in Jeddah and showed a picture of two NGCs on 'internal' work. This was reported in Book 1 in some detail. The article mentions 'a number' of steel-cabbed export model ERFs, so clearly there were more than the two photographed. It is now known that this subsidiary lasted only from 1976 to 1983, when much of the work and several B-series ERFs passed to Trans Arabia. The vehicles were broken up for parts. This picture was taken by an overland Bromilow driver.

It could be that this chassis was being readied at Sandbach to become one of the five tractive units with 5.34-metre wheelbases that were supplied to Falcon Freight's Jeddah operation. Bill Fitzsimons, who worked for ERF as a field engineer, told me that these were basically the same as the draw-bar outfits supplied to Belgium and France, but they were given fifth wheels and worked as artics. The reason for this was more to do with paperwork than practical concerns!

However, it is more likely that it shows the chassis of one of the eight or so NGC draw-bar outfits, five of which were supplied to France.

(Photo: POD Robinson)

Of these, two were spotted (but never snapped) by the Italian truck photographer Alberto Pesanti. The third went to Michel Jacequemin in Chalons-sur-Marne, the fourth went to La Fleche Marseillaise in La Talaudiere (dept. 42), and the fifth went to Gentiluccy of Villeneuve la Garenne in Paris. The sixth went to Roland Dussaillant in Voiron (dept. 38). The seventh went to Thibault of Stree in Belgium. The wrecker, Q824 RGC (pictured earlier), may or may not be one of these but was more likely to have been a pre-production model and would therefore count as the eighth.

(Artwork by Manal Maseras)

ERF NGCS IN ART

PART 1: MODELS

In this section I exhibit artwork by admirers of the NGC. I have included models because they are akin to sculptures: indeed, if Ashley Coghill's admirable model isn't art, then I'm not sure what is!

The Dutch manufacturer PKC is planning a very detailed, high-quality white metal kit of the NGC in 1:50 scale. The 4x2 tractive unit will be a mixture of die-cast, white metal and resin parts, and it should be available sometime during 2019.

(Photo: Frank Waller)

The pictured 1:76 scale model was launched by Road Transport Images in June 2016. Commissioned by Neil Johnston, it was produced by Frank Waller of RTI in plastic kit form. The exhibition models bore Beresford Transport livery and the correct registration plates, the nearest being GEH 513N, which briefly undertook Middle East work and was operated by a sub-contractor.

(Photo: Robert Hackford)

Another of Frank Waller's creations, this time a model of the demonstrator, JLG 35N, that was sold in Kuwait after completing a Middle East tour in the hands of ERF's field engineer Bill Fitzsimons. Frank also prepared the trailer.

This prize-winning 1:24 scale model was crafted by Ashley Coghill. It is an entirely unique representation of one of Eric Vick's NGCs. Lorry restorers and model builders may be interested to know that the base

(Photo: Ashley Coghill)

colours for the Eric Vick livery were International Red (chassis), and Moroccan Maroon (cab).

PART 2: GRAPHICS

(Artwork by Robert Hackford)

This is hardly art: more of an idle doodle! I made it when I first conceived the idea of starting a project in pursuit of knowledge about ERF NGCs in spring 2012, when I was working in Cairo. There was a wonderful garden restaurant/bar that I frequented regularly. It even had a grand piano, which I occasionally played myself upon request. Sitting there under the palms among the spilling bougainvillea and tinkling fountains, I would sip cold beer after a long day at school and ponder on favourite trucks from my driving days whilst trying to calculate what my theoretical favourite '70s unit would be, first and foremost as a driver. The author was presented with this model in 2018.

I was absolutely scrupulous in my quest to marginalise any notions of choosing a favourite tractive unit from the viewpoint of a haulier, a haulier's accountant, a transport enthusiast or an engineer. However, having been an owner–driver, it wasn't difficult to recognise the NGC as a winner for the international one-man operator. It was there and then in Cairo, as I dusted off the mental haze of a school day, with the blood of road haulage still coursing distantly through my veins, that I realized what a wonderful model the almost forgotten NGC was. However, I knew very little about its wider history, so I started to research online and in available books. I needed to network with others who knew about NGCs. In this way, my project started.

The Finnish truck artist 'Benkku' spotted online a picture of the artic I once operated and produced this pleasing impression of what an NGC might have looked like in my colours!

(Artwork by 'Benkku')

The rather impressive piece of artwork shown here was created by a Spanish transport artist called Manal Maseras. It is actually a picture of Beresford's JDF 123N, probably based on Roy Mead's photograph

(Artwork by Manal Maseras)

in the first *Lorries of Arabia* volume; but Manal has given it a fictitious number ending in M. In reality, NGCs were not available to UK operators during the 'M' period! I love the way he has used the light and added little details, like lining out the wheels and mudguard in white, silvering the ERF badge, moving the TIR plate to the bumper and placing iodined fog lamps under the bumper.

These three drawings by the Dutch transport historian Hans Witte show the progression of the NGC throughout its five-year production run from the beginning of 1973 to the end of 1977. Indeed, this contributor provides the rest of the artwork for this section. His photograph of the NGC displayed at the 1975 Brussels motor show appears in the European section of this book. Hans was impressed with what he described as a 'mighty, sturdy and powerful truck' and he has had a soft spot for them ever since. 'In my opinion,' he says, 'ERF was one of the British manufacturers who reacted to the market better: develop a good, sturdy, comfy and reliable European truck and sell it abroad. So instead of criticism, Peter Foden and his crew should be honoured for their vision and daring competition in Europe.' Praise indeed. 'For me,' Hans says, 'the ERF European is the best product that the British truck industry has ever made. An iconic truck and one of my all-time favourites.'

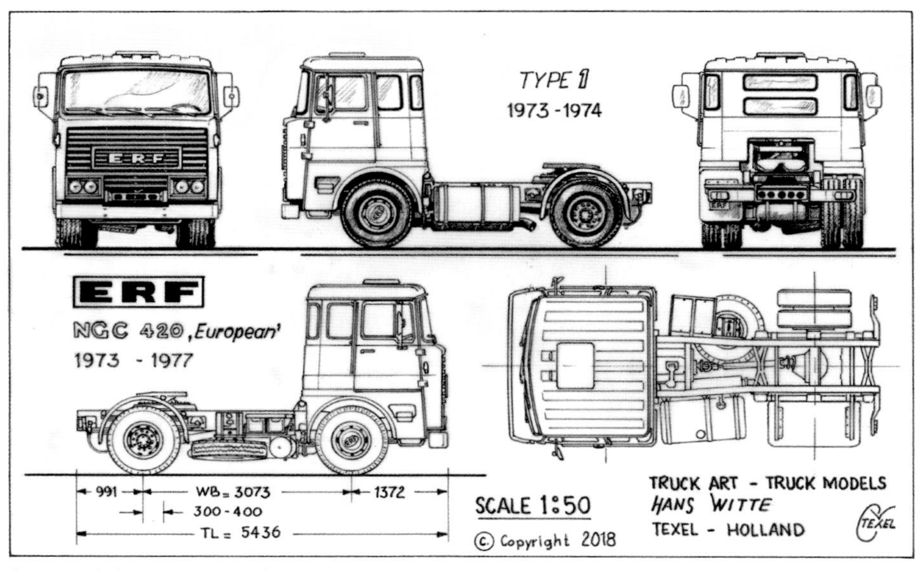

(Artwork by Hans Witte)

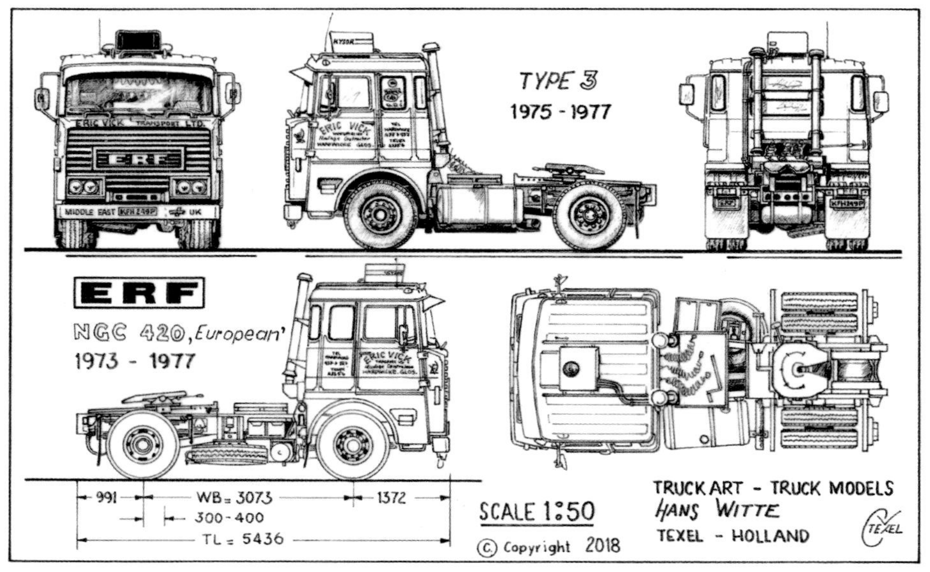

(Artwork by Hans Witte)

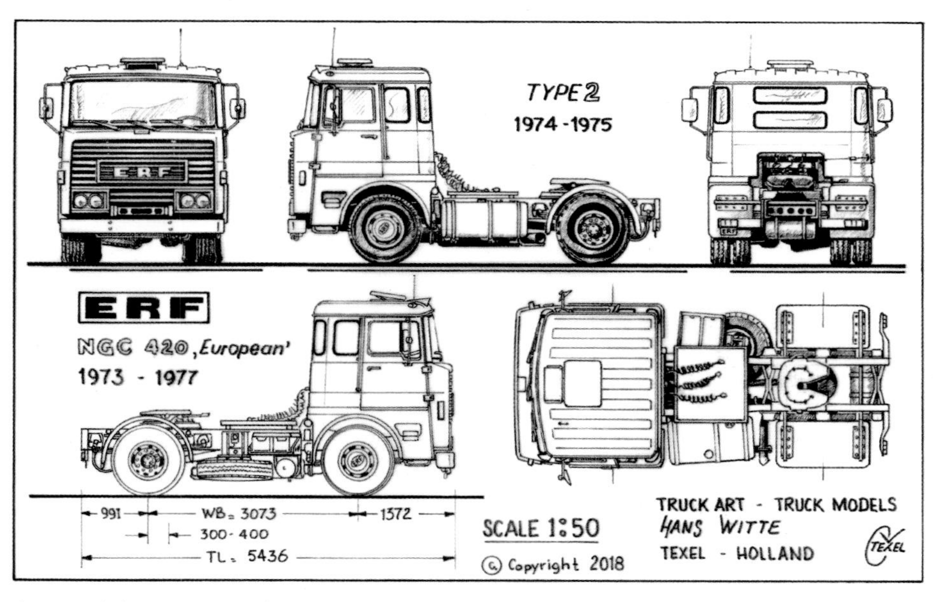

(Artwork by Hans Witte)

(Artwork by Hans Witte)

Here Hans has caught the rugged atmosphere of a Trans Arabia NGC on road-train duties in Saudi Arabia. These ERFs performed extraordinarily well in this harsh environment. The unit is identifiable as fleet number 142, which started life as KFH 248P in Eric Vick livery.

Another NGC on Middle East work. This painting shows JLG 35N before its journey to Lebanon, Syria, Jordan, Saudi Arabia, Qatar and

(Artwork by Hans Witte)

Kuwait. Its oriental venture is described in more detail in the Middle East section of this book.

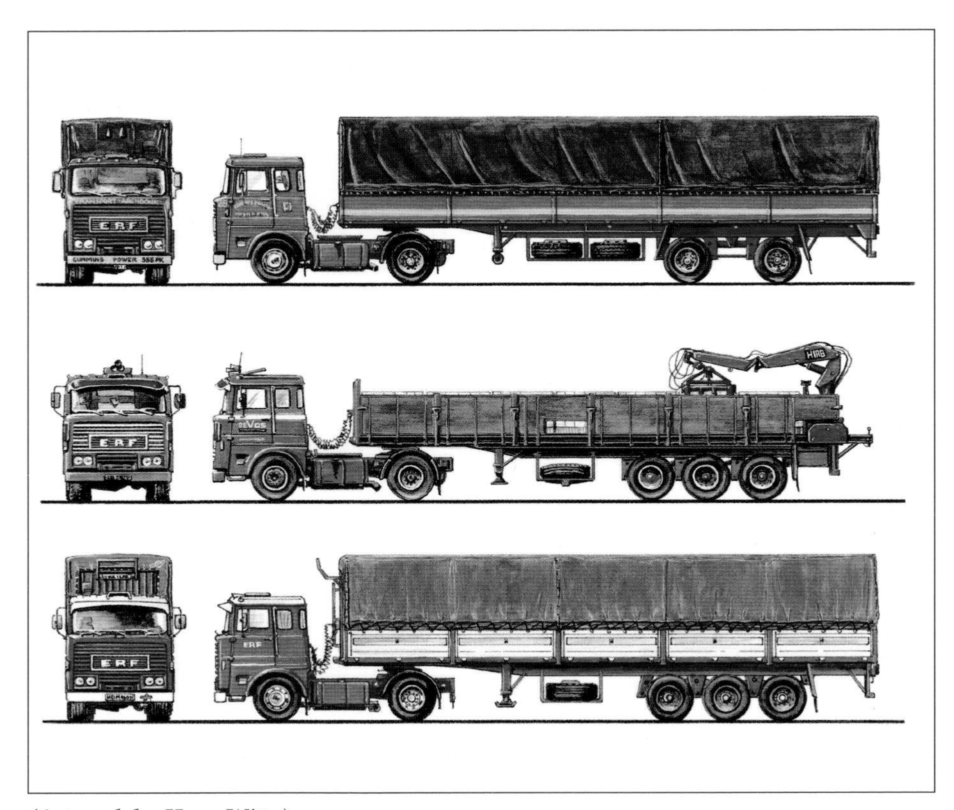

(Artwork by Hans Witte)

In this set of drawings, the first NGC can be seen in the livery of Van Steenbergen (Belgium), registration number AFU.615. This was a very early NGC still without the filler cap and with square top marker lights. The second drawing shows Rien de Vos (Holland) registration number 21-96-NB. Hans reminds us that the trailer was a tri-axle with double wheels and that the outfit ran at 45 tonnes gross. It was one of a pair operated from Goudswaard.

The bottom picture depicts the ERF registration number KDM 460N, which served as the demonstrator on Pat Kennett's 1975 Euro-test.

(Artwork by Hans Witte)

The top drawing in this last set shows an NGC affectionately known as 'The Bear'. It was operated by Cees Willemstein (Holland) registration number DB-77-52. Photos show this vehicle with panels covering the slatted front grille, a sort of customising not uncommon in the Netherlands around 1980.

The Groenenboom (Holland) NGC in the middle bore registration number 12-97-FB and featured in the test conducted by *Bedrijfsvervoer* magazine in September 1975. The load consisted of 20 Stelcon concrete slabs, each weighing 1.5 tonnes. Its gross weight was 41.5 tonnes for the test.

Lastly, a drawing of the beast operated by Marcel Eyckmans (Belgium) registration number 7DF.44. Hans points out that the placing of the Fassi crane so far aft of the cab was to help distribute its heavy weight to avoid overloading the front axle. 'As far as I can see from the pics,' Hans told me, 'the tank for the hydraulic oil is on the right behind the cab with the tool box to the left of it. The big crane needed a lot of oil to operate. With a full load of timber the GTW must have been around 45 to 50 tonnes.'

(Photo: ERF promo)

LATE NEWS

For a transport historian new material will always come to light, so I am squeezing in these two late entries below, just before the book goes to press.

(Photo: Werner Pap NL collection)

In a new publication by Werner Pap, *100 Years of Transport Around Dordrecht*, this picture of DB-77-52 appears in the livery of Piet Kooy, who ordered it on the spot when he saw the newly launched ERF NGC exhibited at the Brussels Motor Show. He fitted it with a night heater, which was unusual for those days, and gave it an early version of a trailer with air suspension. Werner was so impressed with the pulling power of the Cummins that he called his ERF 'de locomotief'!

(Photo: ERF promo)

NGCs fitted with the Cummins 335 had a 9-speed Fuller box. It is worth noting that the Fuller RT 9509 and 9509A used in NGCs were direct-top gearboxes with slightly different ratios; and that these followed the normal H-pattern shift. RTO versions had overdrive-top and followed a U-shaped shift pattern within the H-shape layout. The 13-speed version that came with the Cummins 290-powered NGCs tended to be RTOs.

FINALE

(ERF advert)

Finally, you may remember how, in the closing pages of Book 1, we imagined together the progress of a long-haul NGC driver heading for the Orient. Well, let us pick him up once again as he wends his way through Turkey in mid-winter. He lets in the clutch as the traffic moves again and edges round the numerous ice-filled potholes that serve as a road surface in this desolate Turkish town. Snow flurries scatter at the triple wipers' sweep. Effecting another upshift, our driver dodges the teenaged *simit* sellers standing in the road. Piles of sooty snow line the high street and dim bulbs pin-prick the gloom of bleak grey concrete shops. Smoke from open-fronted kebab kiosks billows across the jostling traffic. Thrusting white minarets punctuate the townscape against a foreboding slate sky. Cars push in where they can.

It is snowing heavily by the time the road begins to open out as we clear the suburbs and the grimy ERF and tilt trailer start to climb. Our driver decides to eschew the use of snow chains for now and see if the diff-lock will get him up the hill. Even the beat of the Cummins seems muffled as we climb higher and higher among the hushed fir trees. The bends are gentle enough to cause no serious loss of traction. At the summit we manage to squeeze past a stranded Bulgarian truck and find ourselves at the crest of a steep descent with a glacial surface and a sheer drop to the right. Headlights are reflected menacingly from the ice. Lorries are jammed nose to tail up the narrow hill in the opposite direction.

Disengaging the diff-lock and engaging first gear, the driver nerves himself for the ordeal. The ERF creeps forward and inches down the hillside. He knows he must resist the temptation to use the Jake Brake. Becoming at one with the ERF, his taut body seems to weld itself to the steering wheel and to the footbrake, which he barely touches. Weary drivers mill about in the road. If our driver halts, the trailer will begin to slide sideways down the camber towards the drop; or, where the camber is adverse, towards vulnerable mirrors and crushable cabs; or slide forwards to jack-knife and create a hopeless blockage. It is a horror scenario and the lorries on the first bend are cleared by millimetres. The next descent is steeper and the ERF begins just a hint of a slide. Steering perilously close to the edge to steer out of the slide, our driver nearly drops a wheel over the edge but straightens in time to complete the murderous descent; and steadfastly to commence his next battle with the treacherous road surfaces ahead. He knows that if he can keep his nerve, his sure-footed ERF NGC will not let him down. And it doesn't.

REVISED ERF NGC REGISTER

A word of caution! We know 91 NGCs were built. More than that number of NGCs is listed in the register below. However, it is possible that one or two of those listed may inadvertently appear twice. An obvious example is where a unit without either a registration plate or a known chassis number may have been listed again as a known fleet vehicle. In most cases those necessary links have already been made as a result of research and previously twice-listed units have been combined under a single number. Furthermore, the number of pre-production models is not known; and these may not be among the 91 dispatched from ERF. We may never know if all 91 NGCs are fully accounted for.

My ID No.	Reg. No.	Country of origin plate	Known engine & gear box	Livery/Co	pic?	Year	Axle config.	Comments
01	N-O3-66/34-UB-99/91-99-HB (re-registered in '80)	NL	NTC 335	Vermeulen, Nieuwerkerk a.d. Ijssel	y	'76	4x2	Michelin men, air horn, beacon, uitzonderlijk vervoer (exceptional transport) plate
02	05-17-FB	NL	NTC 335	Vermeulen, Nieuwerkerk a.d. Ijssel	y	'75	4x2	Beacon, Michelin men, 326PK bumper
03	87-69-RB	NL	NTC 335	Willemstein, Barendrecht (till '81); De Regt, Nieuwerkerk (till '82); Vermeulen, Nieuwerkerk	y	'76	4x2	Was run in Goodkoop de Geus livery by Willemstein, then Nabek livery by De Regt
04	KFH 248P/ TA 142	GB/KSA	NTC 335/ Fuller 9	Eric Vick, Hardwicke; Goldings Heavy Haulage, Wootton-Under-Edge; Trans Arabia, Jeddah (late '82)	y	'75	4x2	Air-con, visor, UK – Middle East on bumper, twin breather pipes
05	KFH 249P/ TA 143	GB/KSA	NTC 335/ Fuller 9	Eric Vick, Hardwicke; Goldings Heavy Haulage, Wootton-Under-Edge; Trans Arabia, Jeddah (late '82)	y	'75	4x2	Air-con, visor, Middle East – UK on bumper, twin breather pipes

My ID No.	Reg. No.	Country of origin plate	Known engine & gear box	Livery/Co	pic?	Year	Axle config.	Comments
06	KFH 250P	GB	NTC 335/ Fuller 9	Richard Read, Longhope	y	'75	4x2	Striped bumper, air-con, TIR plate, visor, twin breather pipes
07	NFH 120P	GB	NTC 290/ Fuller 13	Tony Jones, Sandbach (VIJORE livery); Richard Read, Longhope	y	'75	4x2	Pair of stone-guarded bottom spots, striped bumper later
08	7DF 44 / KCH 95N	B/GB	Cummins 335; left factory with Fuller RT 9508A but supplied with 13-sp Fuller RTO9513	Marcel Eyckmans, Betekom; M. Corbishley, Uttoxeter	y	24 May '74	4x2 later convert-ed to 6x4	Chassis no. 27271. Retro-fitted with Rockwell-Hendrickson double-drive and Trilex wheels, stack, & Fassi crane
09	GEH 513N	GB	NTC 335/ Fuller 9, later Fuller 13	Albert Dale/Beresford, Stoke; John Simmons	y	'74	4x2	Chassis no. 28658, stack, twin breather pipes – did Middle East
10	GDS 543N	GB		Thomas Greer & Sons, Holytown	y		4x2	Striped bumper
11	HNV 59N	GB	NTE 290	Cummins, New Malden; Vee & Inline Diesels, Daventry; Pountains, Sudbury; Watts Trucks, Newport; Redcap Transport, Newport; Jona Haulage	y	'74	4x2	NGC 420 but with 290 big cam Cummins Chassis no. 29069 (for training trailer)

My ID No.	Reg. No.	Country of origin plate	Known engine & gear box	Livery/Co	pic?	Year	Axle config.	Comments
12	4644FX94	F		La Fleche Marseillaise, La Talaudiere (dept. 42)	y		4x2	Draw-bar tilt
13	ZH 120 919	CH	NTC 335	Hans Burkhard, Zurich	y	'74	4x2	Visor
14		CH		Hans Burkhard	y		4x2	Did Middle East work
15	7681RR91	F		(White and orange)	y		4x2	-
16	1557 PF89	F	NTC 290/ Fuller 13 (9513)	R. Collin Exploitation Foresterie, 89 Montillet	y		4x2	Still intact though derelict
17	DEA044 (no. 21)	B	NTC 335/ Fuller 9	Van Steenbergen, Arendonk	y	'75	4x2	Visor
18	324BO (no. 10)	B	NTC 335/ Fuller 9	Van Steenbergen, Arendonk	y	'73	4x2	Visor
19	1HY84 (no. 16)	B	NTC 335/ Fuller 9	Van Steenbergen, Arendonk	y	'74	4x2	Visor
20	AFU615 (no. 28, later 31)	B	NTC 335/ Fuller RTO 9509A	Van Steenbergen, Arendonk	y	'74	4x2	Chassis no. 22993, visor
21	134D8 (no. 09)	B	NTC 335/ Fuller 9	Van Steenbergen, Arendonk	y	'73	4x2	Visor
22	L423R (no. 19)	B	NTC 335/ Fuller 9	Van Steenbergen, Arendonk	y	'75	4x2	Visor
23	Fleet no. TA 106	KSA	NTC 290/ Fuller 13	(New to) Trans Arabia, Jeddah	y		4x2	

My ID No.	Reg. No.	Country of origin plate	Known engine & gear box	Livery/Co	pic?	Year	Axle config.	Comments
24	Fleet no. TA 108	KSA	NTC 290/ Fuller 13	(New to) Trans Arabia, Jeddah	y		4x2	Air horn, striped bumper, Arab decorations
25	Fleet no. TA 110	KSA	NTC 290/ Fuller 13	(New to) Trans Arabia, Jeddah	y		4x2	Air horns, air-con
26	Fleet no. TA 124	NL/KSA	NTC 335/ Fuller 9	Trans Arabia, Jeddah	y		4x2	Ex-NL
27	KDM 460N	GB	NTC 335/ Fuller 9	ERF, Sandbach (Trans Europe test)	y	'75	4x2	Visor. 335/9 sp
28		B	NTC 335/ Fuller 13	De Meule-meester, Pittem	y		4x2	Chassis no. 27979
29	KFH 251P	GB	NTC 335/ Fuller 9	Richard Read, Longhope	y	'75	4x2	Visor, Kaisor air-con. Later converted to RHD and received a B-series day cab
30	(N-11-20) 12-97-FB/TA 139	NL/KSA	NTC 335/ Fuller 9	Groenenboom, Ridderkerk (till '77); Steef Slappendel; Trans Arabia	y		4x2	Acquired by Trans Arabia from Steef Slappendel in Jeddah
31	(N-06-55) 41-54-NB	NL	NTC 335 Fuller 9	Barend Sjouw, Portugaal	y	'76	4x2	Ex-demo at Amsterdam show '76
32	Fleet no. TA 105	KSA	NTC 290/ Fuller 13	(New to) Trans Arabia, Jeddah	y		4x2	
33	Fleet no. TA 109	KSA	NTC 290/ Fuller 13	(New to) Trans Arabia, Jeddah	y		4x2	
34	5673KH59	F	NTC 335/ Fuller 9	Loste, Hellemmes-Lille	y		4x2	

My ID No.	Reg. No.	Country of origin plate	Known engine & gear box	Livery/Co	pic?	Year	Axle config.	Comments
35		F/B		Luff Transport Ltd (LTL)	y		4x2	Briefly with LTL in Comart livery; then sold to Belgian operator
36	JJ393	B	NTC 335/ Fuller RTO909A	Thibaut, Stree (ex-ERF demo)	y	'73	4x2	Draw-bar outfit Chassis no. 24684 Engine 51900
37	JLG 35N	GB/KWT	NTC 335/ Fuller 9	ERF, Sandbach demo; an operator in Kuwait	y	'74	4x2	Air-con, visor, breather pipes. Sent out as Middle East demonstrator
38	2758W92	F		Laiteries Preval, Vire	y		4x2	Demonstrator
39	MMG 772P	GB	NTC 335/ Fuller 9	A.J. Bradick, Leyton (London); GL Baker, Faversham, then Silvertown	y	'75	4x2	GL Baker fleet no. 792
40	7650DA93	F			y	'74	4x2	Not sign-written
41	7011KG78	F		Mentre, Yvelines	y	'74	4x2	
42	8814GV59	F	NTC 335/ Fuller 9	Loste, Hellemmes-Lille	y	'75	4x2	
43	3987RM50	F			y	'75	4x2	Not sign-written
44	813AMH75	F			y	'75	4x2	Did Middle East work
45	DB-77-52	NL		Kooij, Hendrik-Ido-Ambacht; Willemstein, Barendrecht	y	'74	4x2	Completed 1.3 million km before being sold to a breaker in 1989 still in H.T. Wilhelminakade livery

My ID No.	Reg. No.	Country of origin plate	Known engine & gear box	Livery/Co	pic?	Year	Axle config.	Comments
46	16-37-FB	NL	NTC 335	Groen, Nieuw Lekkerland (till '82)	y	'74	4x2	Was demonstrator at the 1974 RAI show in Amsterdam Chassis no. 28095 Registered in NL 19 September 1974
47	83-75-HB	NL	NTC 335	Rien De Vos, Goudswaard (till '79)	y	'76	4x2	440,000 km on the clock: no major probs
48	(N-06-00) 21-96-NB	NL	NTC 335	Rien De Vos, Goudswaard (till '80)	y	'76	4x2	
49	(N-11-48) 06-09-TB	NL		Groenenboom, Ridderkerk	y	'77	4x2	
50		UAE	NTC 335	Falcon Freight, Dubai	y	'75/76	4x2	
51		UAE	NTC 335	Falcon Freight, Dubai	y	'75/76	4x2	
52		UAE	NTC 335	Falcon Freight, Dubai	y	'75/6	4x2	
53		UAE	NTC 335	Falcon Freight, Dubai	y	'75/6	4x2	
54		UAE	NTC 335	Falcon Freight, Dubai	y	'75/6	4x2	
55	KRH 153P	GB	Cummins NHC 250 NTC 335/ Fuller 9; then Cummins 350/Fuller 13 /coach diff	Ted Croswell; PG Horridge, Poole	y		4x2	TIR plate, visor
56		B			y		4x2	CDB demonstrator. Red with white band

My ID No.	Reg. No.	Country of origin plate	Known engine & gear box	Livery/Co	pic?	Year	Axle config.	Comments
57		KSA	NTC 335/ Fuller 9	Cunard Arabian Middle East Line (CAMEL), Jeddah	y		4x2	
58		KSA	NTC 335/ Fuller 9	Cunard Arabian Middle East Line (CAMEL), Jeddah	y		4x2	
59		F		Transports Gentiluccy Freres, Gennevillier/Villeneuve La Garenne (Paris)	y		4x2	Draw-bar tilt
60	BER.329	B		Transports Gruwez, Brugge	y			Red plastic visor
61		KSA		Falcon Freight, Jeddah		'75/76	4x2	5.34 m w/b
62		KSA		Falcon Freight, Jeddah		'75/76	4x2	5.34 m w/b
63		KSA		Falcon Freight, Jeddah		'75/76	4x2	5.34 m w/b
64		KSA		Falcon Freight, Jeddah		'75/76	4x2	5.34 m w/b
65		KSA	Cummins NTE 290/ Fuller RT 9509A	Falcon Freight, Jeddah		Dec 1977	4x2	Chassis no. 31927. Last ever ERF MW 5.34 m w/b
66	785AHD75	F		Meffre & Patalacci	y			
67	8264RW95	F	Cummins 335	Cauvas, Bonneuil en France	y	'75	4x2 converted to 6x4	

My ID No.	Reg. No.	Country of origin plate	Known engine & gear box	Livery/Co	pic?	Year	Axle config.	Comments
68	(X-03-44)/84-56-JB Fleet no. TA 126	NL/KSA	NTC 290/ Fuller 13	Schaap, Rotterdam; Trans Arabia, Jeddah	y			Ben Schaap later ran it in the livery of Konig. ADR compliant
69	JDF 132N/ Trans Arabia 125	GB/KSA	NTC 335/ Fuller 9	On lease to Grocott from ERF (Beech's Garage, Stoke); Beresford, Stoke; Trans Arabia, Jeddah	y	'74	4x2	Did Middle East work with Grocott. For a period, Beresford placed it on French plates and based it at Le Havre
70	PDF 444R/ Q691 NTR	GB	Cummins 335/Fuller 9	Tony Jones, Sandbach (VIJORE livery); Richard Read Longhope; Shamara Heavy Haulage, Southampton; Raynor Plant, Alfreton, Derbyshire; Roger Geesons Scrapyard, Hammersmith, Ripley, Derbyshire	y		4x2 Later: 6x4	Converted to 6x4 by Shamara
71	HMO 220N/	GB		Estra BV, Rotterdam (for Calor Transport)	y		4x2	
72	TA 107	GB	Cummins NTC 290/ Fuller 13	ERF; Trans Arabia, Jeddah	y			Demo for S. Jones: written off in an accident. Supplied new to Trans Arabia with accident damage

My ID No.	Reg. No.	Country of origin plate	Known engine & gear box	Livery/Co	pic?	Year	Axle config.	Comments
73	683ZV75	F			y		4x2	Green, white and cream
74	22-44-??	NL		Rien De Vos, Goudswaard	y		4x2	
75		CH		Ohnemus; M. Knopfli, Regensdorf; a collector, Wetzikon	y		4x2	Blue
76		CH		M. Knopfli, Regensdorf; an owner–driver			4x2	Written off in late '80s
77		F		Brame P., Wintzenheim	y		4x2	Written off and broken for spares
78		F						White draw-bar outfit reported by Italian transport photographer/ historian Alberto Pesanti
79		F						White draw-bar outfit reported by Italian transport photographer/ historian Alberto Pesanti
80		B		Wagner, Jumet Gosseliers				Unconfirmed
81		NL	NTC 335/9-sp Fuller RTO 9509	Probably Prooi, Barendrecht		1977	4x2	Olive green. 3.03 m wheelbase
82		NL		Van Marion? (in Damco/Goedkoop – de Geus livery)			4x2	Conflicting evidence of existence

My ID No.	Reg. No.	Country of origin plate	Known engine & gear box	Livery/Co	pic?	Year	Axle config.	Comments
83		F		Transports Jacquemin, Chalons-sur-Marne (now known as Chalons-en-Champagne)	y		4x2	Two-tone blue draw-bar outfit operated by an owner–driver on Italy/Greece work
84	Q824 RGC	GB		Reliable Recovery Services, London; BFI Recovery	y		4x2	Wrecker: may have been a pre-production draw-bar model
85					y		4x2	Draw-bar chassis/cab [pod pic]
86								Bahrain shunter
87	7583PP89	F	Cummins NHC 250	Ferdom/SNCF	y		4x2	Used to pull railway wagons off rail
88		GB		GL Baker, London (in Van Ommeren livery)				
89					y		4x2	The '74 Earls Court demo
90		KSA		The probable third unit of the CAMEL NGC fleet in Jeddah			4x2	NB We know of the two at 57 and 58 on this list. We know that there were 'a number' of NGCs in the fleet
91		GB		ERF prototype	y		4x2	Distinguishing features include: broader slats behind ERF badge, no sidelights, no vent, no water flap, bubble indicator lens, recess in bumper
92		F		Roland Dussaillant, Voiron (dept 38)			4x2	
93		F	13-sp Fuller	Transport Roland Garbez, 62 Bourlon			4x2	Green with red grille

'FALSE FRIENDS'

Other units that were not NGCs but looked like them. These were all earlier 6x4 models (or in one case, a Pacific) that were retro-fitted with 7MW or 8MW cabs. A description of the 8MW cab can be found in the first section of this book.

My ID No.	Reg. No.	Country of origin plate	Known engine & gear box	Livery/Co	pic?	Year	Axle config.	Comments
F1	3756BT59	F	NT380	Loste, Hellemmes-Lille; Sitca	y		6x4	A Pacific with Mack bogie and retro-fitted 7MW cab
F2	UGE 852R	GB	Cummins 335 then 350/Fuller RTO915	Pountains, Sudbury; J & Y Weir of Fernigair	y	'75	6x4	7MW cab replaced a 6MW cab on this RHD MDC 852 (66CU310) chassis no. 33315
F3	AZC 289	B	Cummins 335/then 350 with Fuller RTO915	Hye, Antwerpen; Cauvas		'71, converted '75	6x4	An MCC 852 (66CU335) supplied to Hye with a 3MW cab. Unconfirmed
F4		B	Cummins 335	Van Driesche, Gent		'71	6x4	An MCC 852 (66CU335) supplied to Van Driesche with a 3MW cab. Unconfirmed

LIST OF NGCS ON MIDDLE EAST WORK

NGC MIDDLE EASTERS

List of NGCs on overland work to the Middle East

KFH 248P Vijore group (GB)
KFH 249P Vijore group (GB)
KFH 250P Vijore group (GB)
KFH 251P Vijore group (GB)
NFH 120P Vijore group (GB)
PDF 444R Vijore group (GB)
GEH 513N Albert Dale/Beresford (GB)
JDF 132N Grocott (leased from Beech's Garage)
JLG 35N ERF demo/export (GB)
n/k* Hans Burkhard (CH)
12-97-FB Slappendel (NL)
813AMH75 n/k (F)

*not known

List of NGCs on 'internals' work in the Middle East

TA 105 Trans Arabia (KSA)
TA 106 Trans Arabia (KSA)
TA 107 Trans Arabia (KSA)
TA 108 Trans Arabia (KSA)
TA 109 Trans Arabia (KSA)
TA 110 Trans Arabia (KSA)
TA 124 Trans Arabia (KSA)
TA 125 Trans Arabia (KSA)
TA 126 Trans Arabia (KSA)
TA 139 Trans Arabia (KSA)
TA 142 Trans Arabia (KSA)

TA 143 Trans Arabia (KSA)
n/k Falcon Freight Dubai (UAE)
n/k Falcon Freight Dubai (UAE)
n/k Falcon Freight Dubai (UAE)
n/k Falcon Freight Dubai (UAE)
n/k Falcon Freight Dubai (UAE)
n/k Falcon Freight Jeddah (KSA)
n/k Falcon Freight Jeddah (KSA)
n/k Falcon Freight Jeddah (KSA)
n/k Falcon Freight Jeddah (KSA)
n/k Falcon Freight Jeddah (KSA)
n/k C.A.M.E.L. Jeddah (KSA)
n/k C.A.M.E.L. Jeddah (KSA)

PUBLICATIONS IN WHICH ERF NGCS ARE FEATURED

BOOKS

Baldwin, Nick (1974) *The Observer's Book of Commercial Vehicles.* Warne, London, UK.

Baldwin, Nick (1979) *Vintage Lorry Annual No. 1.* Marshall, Harris & Baldwin Ltd, London, UK.

Bowers, David (2015) *Beyond the Bosphorus.* 5M Publishing, Sheffield, Yorkshire, UK.

Cany, Francis. *Bahuts de France, (Tome 1).* Editions Cany, France.

Davies, Dai (2009) *ERF, the Inside Story.* Titan Publications, Randburg, South Africa.

Davies, Peter (1994) *The World's Best Oil Engined Lorry: ERF Sixty Years of Truck Building.*

Dyer, Patrick (2015) *ERF B, C, CP & E-series.* 5M Publishing, Sheffield, Yorkshire, UK.

ERF *A-series & MW Workshop Manual TSP 35.* ERF, Sandbach, Cheshire, UK.

ERF (1974) *Manuel de Conducteur* (NGC driver's handbook in French). ERF, Sandbach, Cheshire, UK.

Forbes, Mike (2013) *80 Years of ERF.* Key Publishing Ltd, Stamford, Lincolnshire, UK.

Hackford, Robert (2015) *Lorries of Arabia: ERF NGC.* 5M Publishing, Sheffield, Yorkshire, UK.

Hackford, Robert (2016) *Lorries of Arabia: ERF NGC Part 2.* 5M Publishing, Sheffield, Yorkshire, UK.

Heaton, Paul (2005) *Road Transport and the Read Family.* Heaton Publishing, Abergavenny, Monmouthshire, UK.

Kennett, Pat (1978) *ERF World Trucks No. 1*. Patrick Stevens Ltd, Cambridge, UK.

Littlemore, Alan and Millar, Alan (1993) *60 Years On – the Story of ERF, a British Commercial Vehicle Manufacturer.* ERF Trucks, Sandbach, Cheshire, UK.

Maes, Mario *Transportnostalgie uit Belgie.* Tinne Van Looveren, Sint-Niklaas, Belgium.

Millar, Alan (1986) *Truck Recognition.* Ian Allan, London, UK.

Peck, Colin (2012) *Those Were the Days … British and European Trucks of the 1970s.* Veloce Publishing, Dorchester, Dorset, UK.

Roundoak Publishing, Wellington, Somerset, UK.

Unwin, Ros (2013) *Staffordshire Hauliers Two.* Churnet Valley Books, Leek, Staffordshire, UK.

MAGAZINES

Auto-en-Transportwereld magazine, 18 October 1974 issue (full review of NGC) (Dutch).

Auto-en-Transportwereld magazine, 1 November 1974 issue (NGC advert) (Dutch).

Auto-en-Transportwereld magazine, 5 March 1976 issue (NGC advert) (Dutch).

Bedrijfstransport magazine, December 1974 (NGC test).

Beroepsvervoer magazine, 20 August 1975 issue (account of Truck's Euro Test with NGC) (Dutch).

Beroepsvervoer magazine, 17 September 1975 issue (NGC advert) (Dutch).

Beroepsvervoer magazine, 7 April 1976 issue (NGC mentioned in later Euro Test) (Dutch).

Beroepsvervoer magazine, December 1978 issue (Dutch).

Charge Utile magazine, no. 206, Feb 2010 (French).

Chassis magazine, Issue 20, Spring '74 (NGC feature).

Classic & Vintage Commercials magazine, June 2009 ('Cab Rank' by Peter Davies).

Classic & Vintage Commercials magazine, June 2015 (advert for Lorries of Arabia).

Classic & Vintage Commercials magazine, September 2015 (KCH at Kelsall).

Classic Truck magazine, November/December 2014 (Reitsma French NGC).

Classic Truck magazine, May/June 2015 (advert, Lorries of Arabia).

Classic Truck magazine, June 2016 (book review, Lorries of Arabia 1 & 2).
Classic Truck magazine, May 2018 (article, 'Desert Stormers', includes NGC).
Commercial Motor magazine, 12 January 1973 (motor show NGC).
Commercial Motor magazine, 20 September 1974 (Motor Show).
Commercial Motor magazine, September 1974 (Motor Show Catalogue).
Commercial Motor magazine, 25 April 1975 (whole page NGC advert).
Commercial Motor magazine, 9 May 1975 (table of British tractive units).
Commercial Motor magazine, 26 September 1975 (small note about NGC).
Commercial Motor magazine, 31 October 1975 (Vijore report and picture).
Commercial Motor magazine, 12 January 1980 (small ad, an NGC for sale).
Commercial Motor magazine, 12 May 1984 (ERF exports interview).
Commercial Motor magazine, 28 May 2015 (book preview Lorries of Arabia, full article).
Commercial Vehicle Driver magazine, April 2016 (book review, Lorries of Arabia 2).
Heritage Commercials magazine, January 2011 (NGC in letter about Raynor).
Heritage Commercials magazine, No. 256, April 2011 (Jerry Cooke and Trans Arabia).
Heritage Commercials magazine, No. 311, November 2015 (book review, Lorries of Arabia).
Heritage Commercials magazine, July 2016 (NGC article/book reviews, both Lorries of Arabia).
Heritage Commercials magazine, December 2016 (NGC letter by D.A. Oulton).
Heritage Commercials magazine, December 2016 (NGC letter by R.D. Hackford).
Klassiska Lastbilar magazine, no. 3, 2015 (book review, Lorries of Arabia).
Les Maxis magazine, February 1973 (Belgian – NGC at Brussels show).
Le Poids Lourd magazine, no. 711, September 1974 (French – Paris motor show coverage).
Motor Transport, 20 May 1977 (The Euro ERF: article by Phil Reed).
Motor Transport, 7 July 1978 (CAMEL Jeddah NGCs: article by Alan Bunting).
REVS International magazine, Issue no. 11 (John Simmons on GEH 523N Middle East).
REVS International magazine, Issue no. 16 (Wobbe Reitsma on European NGCs).
REVS International magazine, Issue 32 (sale of GEH 513N).
REVS International magazine, Issue 68 (Flemish ERFs: article by Wobbe Reitsma).

REVS International magazine, Issue 78 (Arabian Knights: article by Jerry Cooke).
REVS International magazine, Issue 83 (illustrated news of Eykmanns sale).
REVS International magazine, Issue 87 (Hefty European: article by Wobbe Reitsma).
REVS International magazine, Issue 104 (European Flyers: article by Wobbe Reitsma)
REVS International magazine, Issue 106 (reference to Pountain's unit).
REVS International magazine, Issue 114 (Reitsma on Jones of Aldridge).
REVS International magazine, Issue 134 (Jona, HNV 59N).
REVS International magazine, Issue 151 (breakdown wagon).
REVS International magazine, Issue 156 (Richard Read).
REVS International magazine, Issue 160 (Wobbe Reitsma).
REVS International magazine, issue 162 (ERF, Sand & Stars: Robert Hackford).
REVS International magazine, Issue 164 (King of the Mountains: Robert Hackford; Eric Vick: Wobbe Reitsma).
REVS International magazine, Issue 165 (two new pictures).
Roadway magazine, February 1973 (launch of NGC 'Euro-Truck')
Speciaal Transport magazine, May 1985 (Dutch – features UGE 852R).
Transmobiel magazine no. 118 vol. 5 December 2004/January 2005 (Dutch).
Transport News magazine, September 2015 (book review, Lorries of Arabia).
Transport News magazine, August 2016 (book review, Lorries of Arabia 2).
TRUCK magazine, November 1974 (NGC on cover and inside).
TRUCK magazine, May 1975 (NGC advert).
TRUCK magazine, June 1975 (Euro Test).
TRUCK magazine, July 1975 (letter from Peter Foden).
TRUCK magazine, December 1975 (Euro Test no. 2 with NGC refs).
TRUCK magazine, January 1976 (looking back over year including the Euro Test).
TRUCK magazine, July 1977 (Euro Test mentions NGC).
TRUCK magazine, August 1977 (Euro Test mentions NGC).
TRUCK magazine, July 1978 (ref to NGC in F12 Euro Test).
TRUCK magazine, April 1981 (Vick/Bandag advert).
TRUCK magazine, December 1992 (Euro Test comparison – Kennett).
TRUCK magazine, July 1996 (piece includes NGCs).
TRUCK & DRIVER magazine, July 1988 (Albert Dale LDD).
TRUCK & DRIVER magazine, June 2015 (book review, Lorries of Arabia).

TRUCK & DRIVER magazine, June 2016 (book review and advert, Lorries of Arabia 2).
TRUCK & DRIVER magazine, March 2018 (Motor Panels article ref Mk 4 7MW).
TRUCKING International magazine, Issue No. 1 1984 (ERF piece mentioning NGCs).
TRUCKING International magazine, December 1986 (The Dutch Connection: article by Niels Jansen).
TRUCKING International magazine, February 1998 (Peter Davies A-series incl. NGCs).
TRUCKING magazine, 376 May 2015 (advert Lorries of Arabia).
TRUCKING magazine, 378 July 2015 (book review, Lorries of Arabia).
TRUCKING magazine, 379 Summer (July) 2015 (book review and article, Lorries of Arabia).
TRUCKING magazine, 390 June 2016 (book review, Lorries of Arabia 2).
Truckstop News magazine, April 2016 (book review, Lorries of Arabia 2).
Vintage Roadscene magazine, September 2015 (book review).
Vintage Roadscene magazine, May 2016 (book review, Lorries of Arabia).

MISCELLANEOUS PAMPHLETS AND BROCHURES

ERF. *Two axle tractor and truck range* ERF sales brochures in various 1970s editions in English, Dutch, Flemish or French.
ERF. *Illustrated Parts Catalogue* ERF, Sandbach, Cheshire, UK.
Graphite Garage, France Routes (one drawing of NGC) (French, undated).
Road Haulage Archives – Issue 9: The Rare Ones, December 2016 ('The ERF Story' chapter), Kelsey Publishing Group.
The ERF Story, Brian Weatherley, Reed Business Publishing (undated pamphlet).
Van Kemenade. Albert-Jan *Tussen de Ritten Door! 1873–1998 – 125 Years* (history of Van Steenbergen Transport Arendonk).

(Photo: Mark Bailey)